FAST FEASTS
ANTON EDELMANN

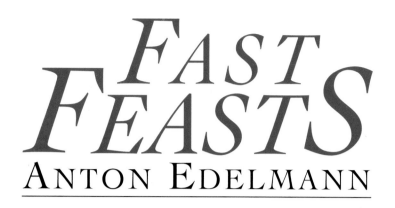

FAST FEASTS

ANTON EDELMANN

TEXT IN ASSOCIATION WITH JANE SUTHERING

RECIPES WITH **MAXIMUM IMPACT**
IN **MINIMUM TIME** FOR **EASY ENTERTAINING**
FROM THE MAITRE CHEF DES CUISINES
AT **THE SAVOY**

HarperCollins*Publishers*

ACKNOWLEDGEMENTS

Nothing good is ever achieved without enthusiasm.
For showing that essential quality in abundance and for their dedication and hard work
I thank all the colleagues and friends who helped me with this book.
My special thanks to the Director and General Manager of the Savoy, Mr Herbert Striessnig
for his help and generosity. My thanks and gratitude to the chefs in the Savoy restaurant kitchen,
especially Paul Cartwright, Tony Hoyle, Nana Yaw Ntiri-Akuffo, Ellen Ritchie
and all the others who showed so much patience, understanding and goodwill.
My secretary, Sophia Petrides, Jane Suthering, with whom this book is my third collaboration,
Barbara Levy and Matthew Solon were all of immeasurable help to me.
My thanks to them, and last, but very far from least, to my wife Sue, for all her tremendous encouragement.

First published in 1995 by HarperCollins Publishers London
Reprinted 1995

Text © Anton Edelmann 1995
Photographs © Gus Filgate 1995
All rights reserved

Anton Edelmann asserts the moral right to be identified as
the author of this work

EDITOR: Jane Suthering
COPY EDITOR: Jane Middleton
TEXT DESIGNER: Joan Curtis
PHOTOGRAPHER: Gus Filgate
HOME ECONOMIST: Jane Suthering
STYLIST: Sue Russell
ILLUSTRATOR: Kiki Lewis
INDEXER: Susan Bosanko

For HarperCollins Publishers
COMMISSIONING EDITOR: Polly Powell
PROJECT EDITOR: Barbara Dixon
DESIGN MANAGER AND ART DIRECTION: Caroline Hill

A catalogue record for this book is available from the British Library

ISBN 0 00 412759 5

Typeset in Cochin
Colour reproductions by Colourscan
Printed and bound in Italy by LEGO spa

FRONT COVER PHOTOGRAPH
Mixed Grill of Atlantic Fish with a Herb Salad, page 124

BACK COVER PHOTOGRAPHS
Brunch: Spiced Red Wine with Fruit and Vanilla Ice Cream, page 32,
Highland Mist with Scottish Raspberries, and Waffles, page 34
Lunch: Summer Menu Three, page 61
Tea: A selection of Sandwiches, pages 101-2, Strawberry Tartlets, page 105,
Pear Frangipane Tarts, and Exotic Fruit Tartlets, page 106
Dinner: Winter Menu Three, page 162

CONTENTS

FOREWORD

I've sometimes said, only half jokingly, that I owe my wife and children to Anton. My wife and I had our first date in the River Restaurant at the Savoy on 19 April 1983, a year after Anton arrived to take charge of the most celebrated hotel kitchens in the world. From first mouthful of canapé (lobster salad) to last cupful of coffee (the Savoy roasts its own), our dinner was a gastronomic triumph. I'm pleased to say it was a romantic one too, aided by courtly service and the wonderful view through the trees of the Thames at night.

The week before my wedding in June 1985, eleven friends and I returned to the Princess Ida Room at the hotel for my stag night – a decorous (no kissograms or exotic dancers) but intemperate affair. We began with tiny baked potatoes stuffed with crème fraîche and topped with a dollop of caviare; no one remembers much else. Later on that evening my gang met up with the wife's hen party (they'd enjoyed a dazzling combination of bingo, cocktails at the Ritz and dinner at Le Caprice). One of my guests fell for one of my wife's guests and they married a year later. So Anton really is responsible for two flourishing marriages and, at current count, five children.

To be the Maître Chef des Cuisines of a great hotel like the Savoy involves much management, much delegation, a great deal of diplomacy and relatively little hands-on cooking. But in spite of being elevated to the culinary purple for thirteen years, Anton has remained a practical and enthusiastic cook at heart. He is lucky enough – as I am – to be the father of girls and he makes time to cook for and with them so he has never lost touch with the way those of us without brigades and walk-in fridges cook. What you will find in this book is the wit, skill and inventiveness of a chef at the top of his class, the recipes made comprehensible and tangible for home cooks without all the time in the world. And running throughout all these dishes – and indeed throughout all of Anton's cooking – is a great sense of the fun and adventure that can be had from making and sharing wonderful food.

Loyd Grossman

INTRODUCTION

'Teach us delight in simple things.'

Rudyard Kipling made that plea for simplicity in a world growing ever more complex. In our own time the pace of change has quickened, and time itself has become a scarce and precious commodity. This book is about using your time to the best possible advantage. By delighting in simple things – readily available ingredients, fresh seasonal produce and straightforward recipes that don't demand culinary gymnastics – *Fast Feasts* shows you how to create first-class food and still have time to savour and enjoy it.

In the Middle Ages, the different professions were known as 'mysteries'. Even today, cooking is often portrayed as something difficult and complicated – an art form demanding special skills, or a science full of secrets known only to the chosen few. Let us begin with a simple definition. Cooking is no more than the preparation of carefully measured ingredients, mixing them together and then heating them for the correct time and at the right temperature. Of course, as with all of life's great pleasures, there is more to cooking than a one-sentence definition. Presentation, the balance of textures and the careful blending of flavours all work together to satisfy our senses.

CHOOSING YOUR **I**NGREDIENTS

I loathe shopping – with the one exception of shopping for food. What has happened in the last ten years is nothing short of a revolution. Supermarkets and small specialist shops now offer us the opportunity to obtain the best ingredients from anywhere in the world.

My rule when shopping for food is to keep it simple. Look for fresh produce that is free from chemicals and other additives and try to stick to the seasons. Produce in its own natural season tastes so much better, and it is usually of higher quality and therefore easier to work with. By shopping with the changing seasons, you bring variety and health to your diet and, just as importantly, you experience the pleasure of the natural cycle of food throughout the year.

Take your time with the selection of food. Spring or summer, autumn or winter, choosing the right ingredients is the basis of all good cooking.

PLANNING YOUR **M**ENU

Look carefully at the balance of the menu you are planning and consider whether the different dishes complement each other. Always choose your main dish first, then your dessert and cheese. If you decide to have cheese, it's entirely up to you whether you serve it before or after dessert. Next you should choose your fish dish or starter. Compare your sauces: if you have a rich sauce for your main course, don't choose a starter with a butter or cream sauce.

In a similar way, think about the different textures in the meal. If you choose a mousse for dessert, don't serve another mousse dish as a starter. What you are trying to achieve is variety and balance.

Try not to repeat the same cooking methods. If you fry the fish, don't fry the meat as well. Ring the changes! You can poach, blanch, marinate, sauté, deep fry, grill, roast, braise, bake or steam. Every choice you make brings a different quality to the food you serve.

Look at the colour of the ingredients, too, and also the temperature. Balance a cold starter with a hot main course and complement your menu with a cold dessert. Try serving a hot dessert if you are having cheese after the main dish.

Then check your menu for repetition of pastry, spices, etc. Try to ensure that each part of the meal has its own distinctive character and identity.

PREPARATION

Even the simplest and shortest recipe benefits from careful planning. Perfection comes from thinking ahead. In this book, most recipes include advice on what you can prepare in advance. I want to leave you with as little as possible to do at the end so you are free to enjoy the food you have cooked!

Every chef will tell you that preparation, '*mise en place*', is just as important as the cooking itself. Gather together the ingredients and all the utensils you will need, making sure you have everything ready before you start. Do not attempt the impossible! Always choose recipes you can cook with confidence. Practice makes perfect, and the more you cook, the more skilled and adventurous you will become. Try cooking the same meal several times. Keep notes and write down exactly what you do so that next time you can make adjustments and improvements, if necessary.

Leave nothing to chance. To make sure you can repeat a favourite dish successfully you need to be precise and accurate in the way you measure and prepare the ingredients. Cooking is about continuous observation and endless curiosity.

SUCCESS

I have cooked countless thousands of meals but I still get a feeling of enormous pleasure every time I see a meal come together. The fish looking fresh and slightly glossy, lightly steamed to just the right texture. The sauce smooth and shiny with a good consistency. The vegetables crisply cooked and deep in colour. The meat juicy and moist, with a light sauce finished perhaps with a knob of unsalted butter. The dessert light, tasty and elegant. And the presentation of everything clear, simple and unfussy.

True success in cooking requires more than just following a recipe. The food you serve is an expression of your personality. Everyone has their own philosophy and approach so do not be afraid to break the rules!

I have worked at the Savoy in exciting times. The great masters of *nouvelle cuisine* led a revolution in creating lighter, healthier and more imaginative dishes. Michel Guérard with his vegetable terrine, Paul Bocuse with his truffle soup, Fredy Giradet with his sea bass in leek – all these chefs broke the rules to create a new surge of enthusiasm and fresh ideas. As with any revolution, not everything in *nouvelle cuisine* has proved to be of lasting value. But the best of the innovations from that time have transformed the way we eat. Interest in food, the skill of professional chefs and the knowledge of people who cook for pleasure at home have all increased in a spectacular way.

I see cooking as one of the threads that bind us to each other and to the past. I owe a great deal to tradition, and I try to learn from everyone I meet who shares my passion for food – my colleagues at the Savoy, my customers, the friends I have made when travelling all over the world, my family, and the people I knew in childhood. Over the last 20 years the list of people who have helped and inspired me is far too long for me to name them here.

Finally, cooking is about pleasure. I hope my fast feasts will bring you pleasure as you create them in your kitchen – and even greater rewards when you sit down in the company of friends to eat and enjoy your labour of love.

NOTES ON THE RECIPES

All recipes serve 4 people unless otherwise indicated.

Eggs: Size 2 eggs are used in all the recipes; free-range eggs should be used where possible.

Herbs: Always chop fresh herbs just before required, to ensure maximum flavour.

Citrus fruits: Use unwaxed fruits whenever possible; if the fruits are waxed, wash and scrub them well and dry before use.

Spoons: British Standard measuring spoons are used in all spoon measurements. These are a 5ml teaspoon and a 15ml tablespoon.

Metrication: A 30g unit has been used as an equivalent weight for 1oz, which is 28.3g.

Gelatine: I use leaf gelatine in preference to powdered gelatine; it is easier to use and dissolves more readily. It is available from good food shops. Four sheets are equivalent to 1 tablespoon powdered gelatine and sufficient to set 600ml/1 pint liquid. Soak the leaves in water to cover for 10 minutes, then squeeze out excess liquid and add the softened gelatine to the warm recipe liquid. It will dissolve almost at once. Powdered gelatine is better soaked in a measured amount of liquid from the recipe, and then needs to be dissolved over the very gentlest of heat. If you are nervous, do this in a bowl set over a saucepan of simmering water. For the bolder cook, heat the gelatine directly in a saucepan.

BRUNCH

Brunch is all about crossing boundaries. It originated in America, a country founded on the idea of the melting pot, of bringing together different influences, ideas and ways of living. Combine the best of breakfast with the best of lunch and you have a wonderfully flexible meal in which you can ring whatever changes you please.

Creativity and choice, mixing and matching, designing a menu that is tailor-made for your guests and for the occasion – that is the secret of a good brunch. As the song says, 'Anything goes.'

Well, almost anything. When I am cooking brunch I let my culinary imagination run free but I do follow some basic rules. The first of these is simplicity. I serve dishes that are simple to prepare and can be presented with the least possible fuss. Secondly, I try not to mix too many flavours together, and restrict each recipe to a minimum of ingredients. I believe in letting each dish speak for itself. Robust, wholesome food works best – with honest flavours, good texture and natural colours.

Serving brunch buffet-style gives your guests the opportunity to choose the meal *they* want. It also helps create an informal, easy-going atmosphere. People may turn up at different times, so choose dishes that can be left on a buffet table without spoiling or becoming tired and past their best.

Brunch is about fun. It's an ideal way to entertain a large number of people, whatever their age. Cutlets, crab cakes and compotes, salads, pancakes and waffles, the recipes in this section give you the chance to experiment, to combine the New World with the Old, a morning meal with a midday feast.

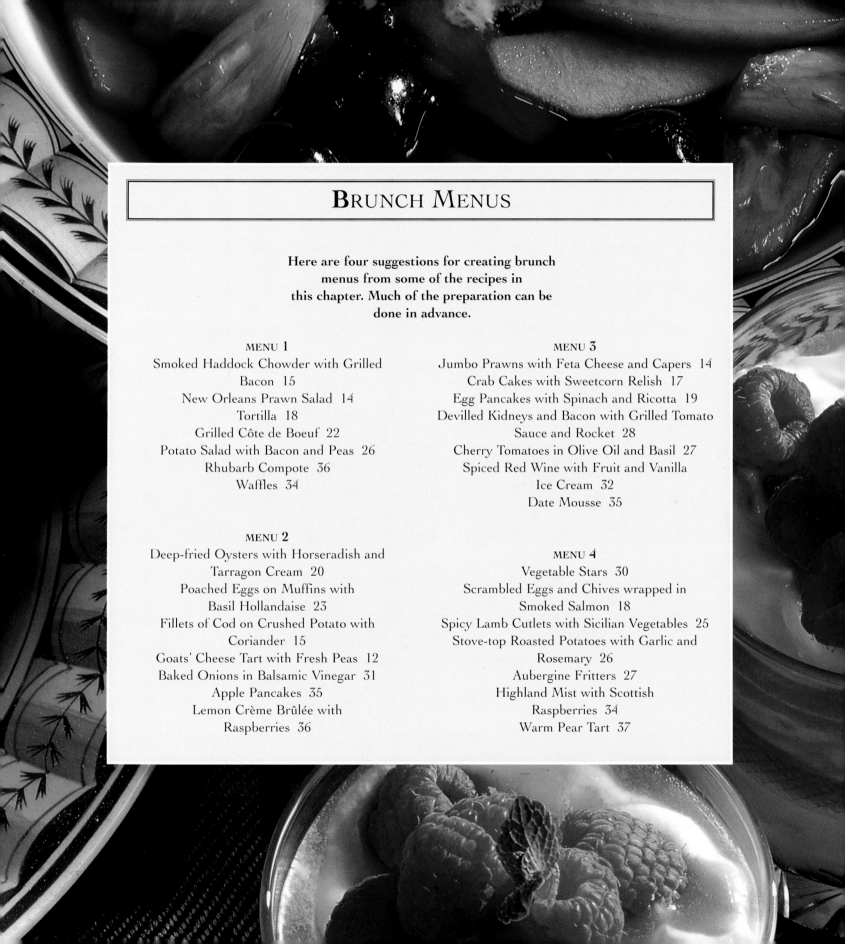

BRUNCH MENUS

Here are four suggestions for creating brunch
menus from some of the recipes in
this chapter. Much of the preparation can be
done in advance.

MENU 1
Smoked Haddock Chowder with Grilled
Bacon 15
New Orleans Prawn Salad 14
Tortilla 18
Grilled Côte de Boeuf 22
Potato Salad with Bacon and Peas 26
Rhubarb Compote 36
Waffles 34

MENU 3
Jumbo Prawns with Feta Cheese and Capers 14
Crab Cakes with Sweetcorn Relish 17
Egg Pancakes with Spinach and Ricotta 19
Devilled Kidneys and Bacon with Grilled Tomato
Sauce and Rocket 28
Cherry Tomatoes in Olive Oil and Basil 27
Spiced Red Wine with Fruit and Vanilla
Ice Cream 32
Date Mousse 35

MENU 2
Deep-fried Oysters with Horseradish and
Tarragon Cream 20
Poached Eggs on Muffins with
Basil Hollandaise 23
Fillets of Cod on Crushed Potato with
Coriander 15
Goats' Cheese Tart with Fresh Peas 12
Baked Onions in Balsamic Vinegar 31
Apple Pancakes 35
Lemon Crème Brûlée with
Raspberries 36

MENU 4
Vegetable Stars 30
Scrambled Eggs and Chives wrapped in
Smoked Salmon 18
Spicy Lamb Cutlets with Sicilian Vegetables 25
Stove-top Roasted Potatoes with Garlic and
Rosemary 26
Aubergine Fritters 27
Highland Mist with Scottish
Raspberries 34
Warm Pear Tart 37

GOATS' CHEESE TART WITH FRESH PEAS

Serves 8

15g (½oz) unsalted butter

1 onion, peeled and finely chopped

450g (1lb) shelled fresh peas

120g (4oz) firm goats' cheese, crumbled

3 eggs

150ml (¼ pint) double cream

Sweet Pepper Sauce (optional)

salt and peppermill

For the pastry

120g (4oz) plain flour

pinch of salt

50g (1¾oz) unsalted butter

45g (1½oz) cream cheese

1 egg yolk, lightly beaten

1 tsp lemon juice

This is delicious served with Sweet Pepper Sauce (see below).

Planning ahead: The tart can be made in advance and reheated.

First make the pastry. Sift the flour into a bowl and add the salt. Rub in the butter and cream cheese until thoroughly incorporated. Add the egg yolk, lemon juice and 1 teaspoon of iced water, then mix to a smooth dough. Roll out the pastry on a lightly floured surface and use to line a 25cm (10 inch) loose-bottomed flan tin or a flan ring set on a baking sheet. Line the pastry case with greaseproof paper and weight it down with baking beans. Rest it in a cool place while you heat the oven to 200°C/400°F/Gas Mark 6. Bake the pastry case for 15 minutes, then remove the paper and beans and bake for a further 5 minutes. Remove from the oven and reduce the temperature to 180°C/350°F/Gas Mark 4.

Melt the butter in a small pan and cook the onion gently until soft and translucent, stirring frequently. Remove from the heat and leave to cool. Blanch the peas in salted water for 1 minute, then drain and refresh in iced water. Spread the onion over the hot pastry case, then add the crumbled cheese and half the peas. Whisk the eggs and cream together and season with salt and pepper. Pour into the pastry case. Bake for 15 minutes, then scatter the remaining peas over the top and bake for a further 25–30 minutes until just set. Serve warm or cold, with the sauce if wished.

SWEET PEPPER SAUCE

Makes about 300ml (½ pint)

8 medium red peppers

120g (4oz) unsalted butter, chilled and diced

salt and peppermill

Cut the peppers in half and remove the core and seeds. Roughly chop the peppers and place in a food processor. Pulse until a fairly smooth purée is formed.

Pass through a fine sieve lined with muslin. Squeeze out the muslin to extract any further juice. You should have a generous 600ml (1 pint).

Pour the liquid into a saucepan and reduce by a generous half by boiling fast. Allow to cool slightly then whisk in the butter a little at a time to thicken and enrich the sauce. Adjust seasoning to taste.

GOATS' CHEESE TART WITH FRESH PEAS ON SWEET PEPPER SAUCE, AND JUMBO PRAWNS WITH FETA CHEESE AND CAPERS (PAGE 14)

NEW ORLEANS PRAWN SALAD

250g (8½oz) cream cheese

4 tbsp crème fraîche

½ red onion, peeled and finely chopped

3 celery sticks, diced

2 tbsp chopped chives

100g (3½oz) peeled prawns, roughly

chopped

1 tbsp lemon juice

1 tbsp white wine vinegar

3 tbsp extra virgin olive oil

handful of mixed lettuce leaves, such as

radicchio, Little Gem, curly endive and

lamb's lettuce

20 cooked king prawns (or Mediterranean

prawns), peeled

salt and peppermill

This is light, refreshing and uncomplicated. Should you be in a slimming mood, use low-fat quark instead of cream cheese.

Mix the cream cheese with the crème fraîche, then stir in the onion, celery, chives, prawns and lemon juice. Whisk together the vinegar and olive oil and toss the lettuce in it, then season with salt and pepper. Arrange the lettuce in a ring on each serving plate, place the cheese mixture in the middle and garnish with the large prawns.

JUMBO PRAWNS WITH FETA CHEESE AND CAPERS

1 onion, peeled and finely chopped

4 tbsp olive oil

2 cloves of garlic, peeled and crushed

6 plum tomatoes, blanched, peeled,

deseeded and diced

100ml (3½fl oz) dry white wine

24 large raw prawns, peeled

120g (4oz) feta cheese, crumbled

1 tbsp capers

2 tbsp chopped coriander

coriander leaves to garnish

salt and peppermill

Sweat the onion in half the olive oil until soft and translucent. Add the garlic and sweat for a further minute. Add the tomatoes and cook for 1 minute, then add half the white wine and cook over a low heat for about 5 minutes, until the sauce thickens. Season with salt and pepper.

Heat the remaining oil in a heavy-based frying pan and fry the prawns over a high heat for about 3 minutes or until lightly browned. Remove from the pan and keep warm. Deglaze the pan with the remaining wine, stirring to soften the sediment, then boil until reduced by two-thirds. Stir in the tomato mixture and then add the prawns, feta cheese and capers. Stir in the chopped coriander and serve at once, garnished with coriander leaves.

SMOKED HADDOCK CHOWDER WITH GRILLED BACON

1 smoked haddock on the bone (see method)

250ml (8fl oz) milk

2 rashers of streaky bacon

30g (1oz) unsalted butter

1 onion, peeled and finely chopped

1 small leek, sliced

2 tbsp plain flour

500ml (16fl oz) chicken or fish stock

1 medium potato, peeled and cut into 6mm
(¼ inch) cubes

2 egg yolks

100ml (3½fl oz) double cream

2 tbsp chopped parsley

salt and peppermill

TIP

This may look as if it has separated, but don't worry – the egg yolks and cream added at the end will put it right.

Planning ahead: The chowder can be prepared in advance to the stage when you add the egg yolks and cream.

Ask your fishmonger to remove the skin and bones from the smoked haddock. Reserve them to flavour the stock.

Bring the milk to the boil and poach the haddock fillets in it for 2 minutes, then lift them out with a slotted spoon and cover with a damp kitchen cloth. Add the skin and bones to the milk and simmer, covered, for 10 minutes. Pass through a fine sieve.

Grill the bacon until very crisp on both sides, then dice or crumble it. Heat the butter and any bacon fat from the grill pan in a heavy-based pan, add the onion and cook until soft and translucent. Add the leek, cover and sweat for about 3 minutes, until soft. Add the flour and cook for 2 minutes, stirring constantly. Stir in the stock and whisk well. Bring to the boil, then add the warm milk and simmer, covered, for 10 minutes. Meanwhile, put the potato cubes in a pan of salted water, bring to the boil and simmer for 10 minutes. Drain and add to the chowder. Just before serving, whisk the egg yolks and cream together with a ladleful of the hot soup and then stir this mixture into the soup. Do not allow it to boil again.

Add the bacon and adjust the seasoning. Place a piece of poached haddock in each soup bowl, pour on the soup and sprinkle with parsley.

FILLETS OF COD ON CRUSHED POTATO WITH CORIANDER

450g (1lb) large firm potatoes, peeled and cut into 2cm (¾ inch) cubes

4 x 120–150g (4–5oz) cod fillets

2 tbsp sunflower oil

100ml (3½fl oz) milk, warmed

4 tbsp olive oil

2 tbsp good-quality white wine vinegar

15g (½oz) bunch of coriander, stalks removed,
leaves chopped

a little lime juice to taste

salt and peppermill

Heat the oven to 200°C/400°F/Gas Mark 6. Cook the potatoes in boiling salted water for about 10 minutes, until just tender, then drain. Season the pieces of cod and fry very quickly in the sunflower oil until well coloured on both sides. Transfer to the oven and bake for about 4 minutes, until cooked through. Keep warm.

Meanwhile, put a third of the hot potatoes through a sieve and mix with the warmed milk, olive oil, vinegar and salt and pepper. Mix the remaining potato cubes and the coriander with this purée.

Place the fish on serving plates, sprinkle with a little lime juice and spoon some potato around each portion.

CRAB CAKES WITH SWEETCORN RELISH, AND SCRAMBLED EGGS AND CHIVES WRAPPED
IN SMOKED SALMON (PAGE 18)

CRAB CAKES WITH SWEETCORN RELISH

200g (7oz) white crab meat

4 eggs, separated

100g (3½oz) peeled prawns, chopped

3 spring onions, finely diced

1 red pepper, deseeded and finely diced

1 green pepper, deseeded and finely diced

15 cocktail gherkins, finely chopped

1 red chilli, deseeded and finely diced

1 tbsp chopped coriander

150g (5oz) fresh white breadcrumbs

plain flour for coating

100ml (3½fl oz) groundnut oil

20g (¾oz) unsalted butter

salt and peppermill

For the relish

2 corn on the cob

4 tbsp caster sugar

juice of 1 lemon

2 tbsp red wine vinegar

1 red onion, peeled and finely chopped

1 red pepper, deseeded and finely diced

1 green pepper, deseeded and finely diced

1 tbsp olive oil

Planning ahead: The crab cakes may be poached or steamed in advance and kept in the fridge for up to 24 hours. The relish can also be made up to 24 hours in advance.

Check the crab meat carefully and remove any shell. Whisk the egg whites until stiff. Fold in the crab meat, prawns, spring onions, red and green peppers, gherkins, chilli, coriander and half the breadcrumbs so that the mixture binds together. Season with salt and pepper. Form the mixture into 8 cakes, wrap each one in cling film and poach or steam for 15–20 minutes, until firm. Leave to cool.

For the relish, cut the kernels from the corn cobs with a small, sharp knife. Put the sugar, lemon juice and vinegar in a small saucepan and bring to the boil, then remove from the heat and leave to cool. Toss the corn, onion and peppers with the olive oil and stir into the cooled liquid. Season to taste.

Lightly beat together the egg yolks. Unwrap the cooled crab cakes and coat them in flour, then in the beaten egg yolk and finally in the remaining breadcrumbs. Reshape the cakes if necessary, pressing the breadcrumbs on firmly. Heat the oil and butter in a heavy-based frying pan and cook the crab cakes for 3–4 minutes, until crisp and golden brown on both sides. Drain on kitchen paper, then serve with the sweetcorn relish on the side.

TIP

As a variation, you can also make these cakes with fish trimmings. They are an ideal brunch or lunch dish.

TORTILLA

4 tbsp olive oil

1 large potato, peeled and cut into slices 6mm (¼ inch) thick

1 onion, peeled and finely chopped

2 cloves of garlic, peeled and crushed

1 red pepper, deseeded and finely sliced

6 eggs

1 tbsp chopped parsley

1 chorizo sausage, peeled and sliced

salt and peppermill

TIP
Tortilla tastes equally good warm or cold.

Heat half the olive oil in a 23–25cm (9–10 inch) non-stick frying pan and fry the potato slices for about 10 minutes, turning occasionally, until softened. Season with salt and pepper and remove from the pan. Add half the remaining oil and the onion to the pan and sweat until soft and translucent. Add the garlic and sweat for a further minute. Add the red pepper and cook for 2 minutes.

Whisk the eggs together and season with salt and pepper, then add the red pepper and onion mixture and the parsley. Heat the remaining oil in the pan and pour in the egg mixture. Stir in the potatoes and chorizo sausage, then cook gently, stirring lightly with a fork, for 3–4 minutes without browning or until the egg starts to set. Pat the surface level and cook for 1 minute without stirring. Slide the tortilla on to a baking sheet, place the pan over the top and turn the tortilla into the pan, cooked side up. Cook the second side for about 3 minutes, until lightly browned. Slide it on to a plate and cut into wedges to serve.

SCRAMBLED EGGS AND CHIVES WRAPPED IN SMOKED SALMON

Serves 4–8

300–350g (10–12oz) smoked salmon, thinly sliced

12 eggs

15g (½oz) chives, chopped

20g (¾oz) unsalted butter

4 tbsp double cream

2 tbsp extra virgin olive oil

1 tbsp sherry vinegar

4 handfuls of mixed lettuce leaves

1 lemon, peeled, all white pith removed, and thinly sliced

sprigs of chervil and edible flowers to garnish (optional)

salt and peppermill

This can also be served as a starter for dinner or supper.

Trim any dark brown areas from the smoked salmon, then use to line 8 small cocotte moulds or ramekin dishes so that it is overhanging the edges of the moulds. Whisk together the eggs, chives and some seasoning. Melt the butter in a heavy-based non-stick pan, add the eggs and cook over a medium heat, stirring constantly with a wooden spoon so the eggs do not stick. When they are nearly set, remove from the heat and add the cream to stop them cooking any further. Continue stirring for 30 seconds, then fill the lined moulds with the scrambled eggs and fold over the smoked salmon. Turn out of the moulds on to heatproof serving plates and place briefly under a preheated grill just to warm the smoked salmon.

Mix together the oil, sherry vinegar and some seasoning. Toss the lettuce leaves in this dressing and serve with the salmon and egg parcels. Garnish with the lemon slices, plus chervil and edible flowers if wished.

FLAT BRIE, BACON AND SAGE OMELETTES

8 rashers of streaky bacon

12 eggs

180g (6oz) ripe Brie, cut into small cubes

150g (5oz) seedless grapes, halved

4 sage leaves, roughly chopped

45g (1½oz) unsalted butter

salt and peppermill

This is indeed a very special omelette. The flavours meld with each other and the sage lifts and intensifies the dish.

Grill the bacon until crisp and then cut it into 1cm (⅓ inch) strips. Whisk together 3 eggs with some salt and pepper, then stir in a quarter of the bacon, Brie, grapes and sage. Heat an eighth of the butter in a 20cm (8 inch) omelette pan until it foams. Add the egg mixture and cook over a moderate heat until just set, shaking the pan lightly and stirring all the time with a fork so that the uncooked egg from the top can flow underneath. Stop stirring for the last 10 seconds so that the omelette can firm up underneath but it should not brown; the centre should be soft and slightly runny. Cover the pan with a plate and turn out the omelette cooked side up. Keep warm while you make 3 more omelettes in the same way. Melt the remaining butter and brush it over the omelettes, then serve at once.

EGG PANCAKES WITH SPINACH AND RICOTTA

4 eggs

2 tbsp chopped herbs

60g (2oz) unsalted butter

100g (3½oz) baby spinach

1 onion, peeled and finely chopped

2 tbsp groundnut oil

1 clove of garlic, peeled and crushed

pinch of nutmeg

100g (3½oz) ricotta cheese, crumbled

20g (¾oz) blanched almonds, roughly chopped

3 plum tomatoes, blanched, peeled, deseeded and diced

Spicy Vegetable Sauce (see page 167)

salt and peppermill

Ricotta can be made from cows' or sheeps' milk. Its flavour and texture make it ideal for fillings and stuffings.

Beat the eggs with the herbs and season with salt and pepper. Heat a knob of the butter in a 20cm (8 inch) non-stick frying pan and pour in an eighth of the egg mixture. Cook for about 30 seconds, then turn and cook the other side for 30 seconds. Make 7 more pancakes in the same way.

Preheat the oven to 180°C/350°F/Gas Mark 4. Pick all the stalks off the spinach and wash twice in plenty of water. Blanch quickly in a large pan of boiling salted water, then drain and refresh in iced water. Squeeze out all the liquid and chop roughly.

Sweat the onion in the oil and remaining butter until translucent. Add the garlic and sweat for a further minute. Add the spinach and heat through, then season with salt, pepper and a little nutmeg. Stir in the ricotta, almonds and tomatoes and heat gently.

Divide the spinach mixture between the egg pancakes and roll them up, then place in an ovenproof dish and warm through in the oven for 15 minutes. Warm the spicy vegetable sauce and serve with the pancakes.

DEEP-FRIED OYSTERS WITH HORSERADISH AND TARRAGON CREAM

24 rock oysters (see method)

1 small shallot, peeled and finely chopped

1 tbsp white wine vinegar

pinch of coarsely ground white pepper

200ml (7fl oz) dry white wine

300ml (½ pint) double cream

50g (1¾oz) fresh horseradish, finely grated

2 tbsp chopped tarragon

vegetable oil for deep frying

3 cloves of garlic, peeled and crushed

a few drops of Tabasco sauce

a few drops of Worcestershire sauce

½ tbsp dried thyme

plain flour for coating

Tempura Batter (see below)

handful of parsley sprigs

salt and peppermill

TIPS

The parsley should be dry when you add it to the oil.

When you open oysters, try and save the juice and add it to the sauce for extra flavour.

Rock oysters are also called Portugese oysters and they are usually much cheaper than their native cousins.

Planning ahead: The sauce can be made up to 4 hours in advance.

You can ask your fishmonger to open the oysters or you can open them yourself. To do this, scrub the shells thoroughly under cold running water. Push an oyster knife into the hinged section of each oyster and twist the knife carefully to remove the flat top shell without touching the oyster flesh. Discard the top shells. Loosen the oysters from the bottom shell, carefully remove the frilly beard around each one and reserve. Store the oysters in the fridge. Scrub the bottom half of each shell and dry it.

Put the shallot, vinegar, white pepper and oyster beards in a small, heavy-based saucepan and boil until reduced by two-thirds. Add the white wine and boil again to reduce by two-thirds. Add the double cream and grated horseradish and simmer until slightly thickened and reduced by about half. Pass through a fine sieve, then stir in the tarragon and season with salt and pepper. Keep the sauce warm.

Heat the oil to about 190°C/375°F. Mix together the garlic, Tabasco, Worcestershire sauce and thyme. Dry the oysters and season them with the garlic mixture, then turn them in the flour until evenly coated, shaking off the excess. Dip in the tempura batter and fry quickly in the oil until golden brown – about 1–2 minutes. Drain on kitchen paper.

Add the parsley sprigs to the oil for about 20 seconds, stirring all the time, until crisp. Drain on kitchen paper. Spoon a little sauce into each shell and top each one with an oyster. Garnish with the deep-fried parsley.

TEMPURA BATTER

2 eggs

120ml (4fl oz) iced water

generous pinch of bicarbonate of soda

60g (2oz) plain flour

Whisk the eggs and water until pale and foamy. Add the bicarbonate of soda and flour and whisk in quickly. Be careful not to overmix; it doesn't matter if the batter is slightly lumpy.

DEEP-FRIED OYSTERS WITH HORSERADISH AND TARRAGON CREAM, AND GRILLED CÔTE DE BOEUF (PAGE 22)

GRILLED CÔTE DE BOEUF

2 x 400g (14oz) beef cutlets, cut off the sirloin

1 tbsp groundnut oil

20g (¾oz) unsalted butter

2 sprigs of rosemary

salt and peppermill

For the chutney

4 red peppers

2 tbsp groundnut oil

1 red onion, peeled and finely chopped

3 cloves of garlic, peeled and finely chopped

1 red chilli, deseeded and finely diced

1 tsp sugar

2 tbsp red wine vinegar

200ml (7fl oz) chicken stock

2 tomatoes, blanched, peeled, deseeded and diced

Planning ahead: The chutney will keep in the fridge for a week. Remove the beef from the fridge about half an hour before cooking, to bring it to room temperature.

For the chutney, cook the red peppers under a preheated grill until blistered and well charred on all sides. Place in a bag and leave until cool enough to handle, then peel, deseed and cut into 1cm (⅓ inch) squares.

Heat the oil in a pan, add the onion and sweat until soft and translucent. Add the garlic and sweat for a further minute. Add the red peppers, chilli and sugar and sweat for 2 minutes. Add the red wine vinegar and boil until reduced by half. Stir in the stock, reduce the heat and simmer until very thick. Add the tomatoes and cook for 3 minutes, stirring frequently. Keep warm.

Season the beef cutlets with salt and pepper. Turn them in the oil and cook under a preheated grill for about 5 minutes on each side, until medium cooked. Leave to rest in a warm place for 15 minutes.

Collect all the juices from the meat. Cut the meat across the grain into 1.5cm (½ inch) slices. Melt the butter in a pan, add the rosemary and heat gently until the butter is golden brown. Pour it over the beef. Add the collected juices to the chutney and serve with the beef.

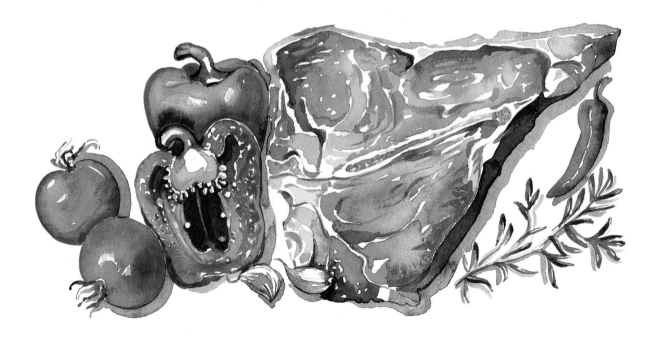

POACHED EGGS ON MUFFINS WITH BASIL HOLLANDAISE

100ml (3½fl oz) white wine vinegar

8 eggs

4 English muffins

8 slices of cooked ham, cut into rounds the
same size as the muffins

For the basil hollandaise

3 Pan-fried Garlic Cloves (see below) (optional)

5 egg yolks

3 tbsp white wine vinegar

100ml (3½fl oz) dry white wine

100ml (3½fl oz) water

½ tsp crushed white peppercorns

1 tsp finely chopped shallot

2 tbsp roughly chopped basil

300g (10oz) unsalted butter

Worcestershire sauce

juice of ½ lemon, or to taste (optional)

salt and peppermill

TIP

Toasted muffins are wonderfully versatile
food for any time of day.

This is my version of a classic brunch dish, Eggs Benedict.

Planning ahead: The poached eggs can be prepared up to 24 hours in advance.

Bring 1 litre (1¾ pints) of water and the vinegar to a simmer in a deep saucepan. Crack each egg into a cup, then slide it gently into the simmering water. Cook for about 3 minutes or until all the egg white has set and closed around the yolk. (You might find it easier to cook the eggs one at a time.) Lift the eggs out of the water and slide them into a bowl of cold water – this will stop them cooking and wash off the taste of vinegar. Drain on kitchen paper, trim off any straggly bits, then cover and set aside.

For the hollandaise, squeeze the pulp from the fried garlic cloves, if using, and mix with the egg yolks. Place the vinegar, wine, water, peppercorns, shallot and a few basil stalks in a saucepan. Boil until reduced by two-thirds and then leave to cool. Pass through a fine sieve and add to the egg yolks. Place in a bain-marie or a bowl set over a pan of hot water and beat with a whisk until the mixture coats the back of a spoon.

Melt the butter slowly and skim the white sediment from the top. Leave to cool to blood temperature – cool enough to put your finger in comfortably – then gradually whisk the butter into the egg mixture. Season with salt, pepper and Worcestershire sauce, plus lemon juice to taste, if using. Stir the basil into the sauce and keep warm.

Cut the muffins in half and toast them under a preheated grill. Top each with a piece of ham and warm this lightly under the grill. Put the eggs in gently simmering salted water just for a minute to heat through, then pat dry with a kitchen cloth and place one on top of each muffin half. Spoon the basil hollandaise over and serve at once.

PAN-FRIED GARLIC CLOVES

1 head of garlic

3 tbsp vegetable oil

30g (1oz) unsalted butter

Separate the cloves of garlic but do not peel them. Cook in boiling salted water until just tender, then drain and dry on a kitchen cloth. Heat the oil and butter in a frying pan and fry the garlic cloves until crisp and golden. They will keep in the fridge for 1–2 weeks if stored covered with vegetable oil.

SPICY LAMB CUTLETS WITH SICILIAN VEGETABLES, AND POTATO SALAD WITH BACON AND PEAS (PAGE 26)

SPICY LAMB CUTLETS WITH SICILIAN VEGETABLES

200ml (7fl oz) olive oil

4 cloves of garlic, peeled and crushed

½ tsp freshly grated ginger

½ tsp marjoram

4 red chillies, deseeded and finely chopped

½ tsp ground caraway seeds

2 tbsp Dijon mustard

1 tsp Worcestershire sauce

8 lamb cutlets, all fat removed

1–2 tbsp black peppercorns, finely crushed

watercress to garnish

Sicilian Vegetables (see below)

salt

These are good served with Aubergine Fritters (see page 27).

Mix together the olive oil, garlic, ginger, marjoram, chillies, caraway seeds, mustard and Worcestershire sauce. Add the lamb cutlets and leave to marinate in the fridge for at least 8 hours or up to 48 hours.

Remove the lamb from the marinade, pat dry and season with salt. Press on the peppercorns in an even coating, then cook under a preheated grill for 2–3 minutes on each side, until well browned but still pink in the centre. Serve lukewarm, garnished with watercress and accompanied by the Sicilian vegetables.

SICILIAN VEGETABLES

2 red peppers

20 pitted Sicilian or Moroccan black olives, sliced lengthways

20 pitted green or picholine olives, sliced lengthways

15g (½oz) bunch of basil, stalks removed, leaves finely shredded

1 tbsp pine kernels, toasted

2 tbsp extra virgin olive oil

½ tsp finely chopped chilli

salt and peppermill

1 Baked Onion in Balsamic Vinegar (see page 31), diced

12 Pan-fried Garlic Cloves (see page 23), diced

Grill the red peppers until charred and blistered on all sides. Place in a bag until cool enough to handle, then peel, deseed and dice. Combine all the ingredients and toss well. Season to taste.

POTATO SALAD WITH BACON AND PEAS

100g (3½oz) shelled fresh peas

600g (1¼lb) new potatoes

4 tbsp chicken stock

1 red onion, peeled and finely chopped

1 clove of garlic, peeled and crushed

100ml (3½fl oz) vegetable oil

4 tbsp white wine vinegar

100g (3½oz) streaky bacon

salt and peppermill

If new potatoes are not available, use King Edwards or Maris Peer.

Boil the peas in salted water until tender, then drain and refresh in iced water. Put the potatoes in a pan of salted water, bring to the boil and cook until tender, then drain. When the potatoes are cool enough to handle, peel and cut into slices 6mm (¼ inch) thick. Keep warm.

Heat the chicken stock and add the onion, garlic, oil and vinegar. Season with salt and pepper and pour over the potatoes, stirring as little as possible to prevent the potatoes breaking up. Grill the bacon until crisp and cut it crossways into 6mm (¼ inch) pieces. Warm the peas in a little salted water, then drain. Sprinkle the hot bacon and the peas over the potato salad just before serving.

STOVE-TOP ROASTED POTATOES WITH GARLIC AND ROSEMARY

900g (2lb) potatoes, peeled and cut into quarters (or, better still, trimmed into barrel shapes 5cm (2 inch) long and 2.5cm (1 inch) wide)

100ml (3½fl oz) vegetable oil

1 garlic clove, peeled and cut in half

2 sprigs of rosemary

20g (¾oz) unsalted butter

salt and peppermill

Planning ahead: This can be prepared up to 2 hours in advance, then gently reheated.

Wash the potatoes well and dry them on a kitchen cloth. Heat the oil in a non-stick pan just large enough to hold the potatoes in a single layer. Add the potatoes and garlic, then cover and cook gently for about 30 minutes without letting them colour too much. When the potatoes are nearly soft, add the rosemary and butter and, if necessary, turn up the heat to colour the potatoes golden brown. Season with salt and pepper and drain the potatoes on kitchen paper before serving.

TIP

Use firm non-floury potatoes such as Craig Royal Reds or King Edwards.

AUBERGINE FRITTERS

500g (1lb 1oz) aubergines

4 tbsp olive oil

1 shallot, peeled and finely chopped

2 cloves of garlic, peeled and crushed

1 tbsp plain flour

1 egg

vegetable oil for shallow frying

salt and peppermill

These go extremely well with lamb or poultry and can be served with yoghurt, crème fraîche or Sweet Pepper Sauce (see page 12).

Preheat the oven to 220°C/425°F/Gas Mark 7. Prick the aubergines all over with a fork, then brush them with some of the olive oil and bake for about 45 minutes or until soft, turning occasionally. Remove from the oven and leave to cool, then cut in half and peel. Place the flesh in a piece of muslin and squeeze out all the liquid. Transfer to a bowl and mash with a fork.

Sweat the shallot in the remaining olive oil until soft and translucent. Add the garlic and sweat for a further minute. Add the shallot mixture, flour and egg to the aubergine purée in the bowl, season with salt and pepper and mix well.

Heat a little vegetable oil in a non-stick frying pan. Place 2 tablespoon quantities of the mixture in heaps in the pan and press down lightly. Fry for about 2 minutes on each side, until golden brown.

CHERRY TOMATOES IN OLIVE OIL AND BASIL

20g (¾oz) unsalted butter

4 tbsp olive oil

500g (1lb 1oz) sweet cherry tomatoes

15g (½oz) bunch of basil, stalks removed, leaves chopped

With hot-house production in Holland and other countries, buying tomatoes has become a pain in the neck. However, if you go on holiday in the Mediterranean you may be lucky enough to find true tomatoes – unevenly shaped, firm yet ripe, with a deep, shiny colour and a flavour full of sun and warm winds. You will never forget the taste.
Providing the tomatoes are sweet, this is an excellent vegetable dish, which could be enhanced with a little sprinkling of freshly grated Parmesan cheese or balsamic vinegar.

Melt the butter in a heavy-based saucepan and add the olive oil. Add the tomatoes and roll them around for 3–4 minutes until heated through. Do not overcook them or they will become mushy. Season with salt and pepper and stir in the basil at the last minute.

TIP
Memo to the Nation: Stop buying tomatoes that can best be compared to unripe apples – terribly acidic, with skin like leather and tough flesh.

DEVILLED KIDNEYS AND BACON WITH GRILLED TOMATO SAUCE AND ROCKET

12 small rashers of smoked streaky bacon

4 lambs' kidneys

1 veal kidney

2 tbsp white breadcrumbs

1 tbsp chopped parsley

2 tsp English mustard

1 tbsp olive oil

½ tsp balsamic vinegar

2 handfuls of rocket

1 tbsp freshly grated Parmesan cheese

For the sauce

2 plum tomatoes

2 green chillies

200ml (7fl oz) double cream

4 Pan-fried Garlic Cloves (see page 23)

salt and peppermill

Cherry Tomatoes in Olive Oil and Basil (see page 27) make a good accompaniment to this dish.

Planning ahead: The sauce can be prepared well in advance.

For the sauce, cut the tomatoes in half, place them on a baking tray skin-side up and sprinkle with salt and pepper. Cook under a preheated grill set at maximum until the skin is black and blistered. Peel off the skin.

Hold the chillies over an open flame (on a gas hob) and turn until the skin is black and blistered. Alternatively, char them under the grill with the tomatoes. Scrape off the skin and remove the seeds and membranes.

Put the double cream in a pan and boil until reduced by half. Put it in a food processor or liquidizer with the tomatoes, chillies and garlic cloves and process to a purée. Adjust the seasoning and reheat.

Grill the bacon until crisp and keep warm. Cut the lambs' kidneys in half and remove the skin from the outside and the fat from the inside. Leave a small layer of fat around the veal kidney and cut it into slices 1cm (⅓ inch) thick. Mix the breadcrumbs and parsley together. Season the kidneys and grill for 2–3 minutes, until well browned on both sides. Brush them with the mustard and sprinkle with the breadcrumb mixture, then return to the grill to brown.

Mix the olive oil and balsamic vinegar together and season with salt and pepper. Add the rocket leaves and Parmesan cheese and toss well. Serve the kidneys and bacon with the rocket salad and hand the sauce separately.

Devilled Kidneys and Bacon with Grilled Tomato Sauce and Rocket, and
Cherry Tomatoes in Olive Oil and Basil (page 27)

VEGETABLE STARS

1 onion, peeled and finely chopped

3 tbsp olive oil

2 cloves of garlic, peeled and crushed

5 rashers of smoked streaky bacon, cut into
fine strips (optional)

4 leeks, cut in half lengthways and
thinly sliced

10 button mushrooms, sliced

1 egg, beaten

20g (¾oz) Home-dried Tomatoes in
Olive Oil (see below)

60g (2oz) Gorgonzola cheese, diced

chopped parsley to garnish

salt and peppermill

For the dough

2 tsp fresh yeast or 1 tsp dried yeast

1 tsp sugar

100ml (3½fl oz) lukewarm water

350g (12oz) strong plain flour

½ tsp salt

3 eggs at room temperature, beaten

3 tbsp crème fraîche

To make the dough, combine the yeast and sugar with the lukewarm water and leave in a warm place for about 10 minutes, until frothy. Mix the flour with the salt in a bowl and make a well in the centre. Pour in the beaten eggs, crème fraîche and yeast mixture. Using a wooden spoon, gradually stir the flour into the liquid ingredients to form a soft dough. Turn out on to a lightly floured surface and knead for 2–3 minutes, until smooth and elastic. Transfer the dough to a lightly buttered bowl, cover with plastic wrap and leave in a warm place for 30–45 minutes, until doubled in size. Punch down the dough with your knuckles and leave it to rest while you prepare the filling.

Sweat the onion in the oil until soft and translucent. Add the garlic and sweat for a further minute, then add the bacon, if using, and fry until crisp. Add the leeks and mushrooms, cover and cook over a gentle heat until soft, stirring frequently. Adjust the seasoning.

On a lightly floured surface, roll out the dough to about 6mm (¼ inch) thick and cut out four 20cm (8 inch) rounds. Brush the edge of each one with the beaten egg, then make 2.5cm (1 inch) cuts at 2.5cm (1 inch) intervals around the edge of the dough. Fold each section over on the diagonal to form small points and press down firmly. Leave to rest in the fridge for 15 minutes. Preheat the oven to 200°C/400°F/Gas Mark 6.

Spoon the filling into the centre of each dough 'star' and brush the points with the beaten egg. Bake for about 15 minutes, then scatter over the dried tomatoes and Gorgonzola and cook for a further 10–15 minutes, until golden. Remove from the oven and sprinkle with parsley.

HOME-DRIED TOMATOES IN OLIVE OIL

plum tomatoes

salt

olive oil

Blanch the plum tomatoes in boiling water, then peel them and cut lengthways in half. Scrape out and discard all the seeds. Cut the halves into 2–3 wedges, depending on size, arrange them on a cooling rack and sprinkle lightly with salt. Leave to dry in a warm place or in the oven on the lowest setting for 12 hours. When dried, the tomatoes will be slightly shrivelled (the salt draws out the moisture, which evaporates in the heat) and a deeper red in colour. Put them in a jar and top up with olive oil. The tomatoes will keep in the fridge for several weeks.

BAKED ONIONS IN BALSAMIC VINEGAR

4 medium red onions, peeled

2 tbsp olive oil

sea salt flakes

100ml (3½fl oz) balsamic vinegar

Preheat the oven to 200°C/400°F/Gas Mark 6. Brush the onions well with the olive oil and sprinkle with sea salt. Bake in a flameproof dish for 45–50 minutes, until tender, then transfer to the hob and add the vinegar, scraping the caramelized juices off the dish. Simmer until the vinegar thickens slightly and the onions are glazed with the sauce. They will keep in the fridge for up to 1 week.

BROAD BEAN AND MINT PURÉE

300g (10oz) shelled broad beans

2 tbsp groundnut oil

45g (1½oz) onion, finely chopped

1 clove of garlic, peeled and crushed

100ml (3½fl oz) dry white wine

200ml (7fl oz) double cream

1 tbsp chopped mint

salt and peppermill

You can use frozen broad beans for this but make sure that they are small ones. It goes well with fish, poultry, veal and pork.

Cook the broad beans in plenty of boiling salted water until tender, then drain, refresh in iced water and peel away the skins. Heat the oil in a heavy-based pan, add the onion and sweat until soft and translucent. Add the garlic and sweat for a further minute. Stir in the wine and boil until reduced by two-thirds, then add the cream and boil until reduced by half. Stir in the broad beans and simmer gently until the cream coats the beans. Transfer to a food processor and process to a rough purée. Season with salt and pepper and stir in the mint. Reheat gently to serve.

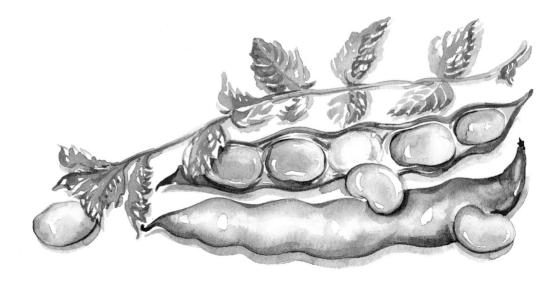

SPICED RED WINE WITH FRUIT AND VANILLA ICE CREAM

400ml (14fl oz) red wine

2 tbsp rum

75g (2½oz) caster sugar

4 cloves

½ cinnamon stick

1 large orange, peeled (reserve the peel) and cut into segments

1 apple, peeled, cored and sliced

1 pear, peeled, cored and sliced

1 small pineapple, peeled, cored and cut into small slices

90g (3oz) grapes

90g (3oz) cherries, stoned

Vanilla Ice Cream (see below)

sprigs of mint to decorate (optional)

My mother used to prepare this dish every Christmas and even little children got a small helping. The smell of the wine and spices still evokes very pleasant childhood memories.

Planning ahead: The ice cream can be prepared at least a day in advance. The fruit can be prepared about 2 hours beforehand and kept covered in orange juice. Drain it well before immersing it in the hot wine.

Heat the wine, rum and sugar in a large saucepan, then add the cloves, cinnamon and half the orange peel. Bring almost to boiling point, then remove from the heat and leave to infuse for about 15 minutes. Remove the spices and orange peel, then add all the fruit and leave to warm through for a few minutes. Ladle into warm soup bowls and top each one with a quenelle (or scoop) of vanilla ice cream. Decorate with sprigs of mint, if using, and serve immediately.

VANILLA ICE CREAM

200ml (7fl oz) milk

200ml (7fl oz) double cream

1 vanilla pod, split and seeds scraped out

6 egg yolks

75g (2½oz) caster sugar

3 tbsp liquid glucose

Put the milk, cream, vanilla pod and seeds in a pan and bring to the boil. Beat the egg yolks with the sugar until pale and thick. Pour the milk mixture on to the yolks, whisking until well blended, then return to the pan and cook over a very gentle heat, stirring continuously, until it is thick enough to coat the back of the spoon. Do not let the mixture boil or it will curdle. Remove from the heat and pass through a fine sieve, then mix in the glucose syrup. Cool the egg custard as quickly as possible – ideally in the fridge. Freeze in an ice-cream machine according to the manufacturer's instructions. Alternatively, pour the mixture into a large freezerproof bowl, cover and freeze until almost set. Transfer to a food processor and whisk until it is creamy and all the ice crystals have broken down. Put the mixture back in the bowl, cover and return to the freezer. Repeat this process twice, then freeze until firm.

SPICED RED WINE WITH FRUIT AND VANILLA ICE CREAM, HIGHLAND MIST WITH SCOTTISH RASPBERRIES, AND WAFFLES (PAGE 34)

HIGHLAND MIST WITH SCOTTISH RASPBERRIES

60g (2oz) plain flour

30g (1oz) caster sugar

45g (1½oz) butter

400ml (14fl oz) double cream

5 tbsp Scottish whisky

140g (4½oz) icing sugar, sifted

200g (7oz) Scottish raspberries

Strawberry Coulis (see page 57)

sprigs of mint to decorate

TIP

Raspberries usually come in 2 crops, with the autumn one producing smaller, sweeter fruit. Any other summer fruit can be used for the Highland Mist.

Planning ahead: The strawberry coulis will keep in the fridge for 2 days if covered with clingfilm. The shortbread can be prepared a day in advance and the cream mixture up to 2 hours in advance.

Heat the oven to 170°C/325°F/Gas Mark 3. Put the flour, sugar and butter in a bowl and work together with your fingertips to form a dough. On a lightly floured surface, roll out to 6mm (¼ inch) thick, then transfer to a baking sheet and bake for about 20 minutes, until pale golden. Allow to cool then break up into small pieces.

Whip the cream with the whisky and, when it is nearly fully whipped, incorporate the icing sugar. Just before serving, fold the shortbread and half the raspberries into the cream mixture and spoon into glasses. Pour a little strawberry coulis on top and decorate with the remaining raspberries and the mint.

WAFFLES

2 eggs, separated

2 tbsp vegetable oil

175ml (6fl oz) milk

100g (3½oz) plain flour

1 tsp baking powder

45g (1½oz) caster sugar

pinch of salt

icing sugar for dusting

Waffles are great things and good fun to make but you might need a bit of practice at judging the correct amount of batter to put in the waffle iron at one time. They go well with fruit compotes, sweet sauces such as raspberry or butterscotch, whipped cream, ice cream and sorbet.

Whisk the egg yolks with the oil and milk. Sift the flour, baking powder, sugar and salt into a bowl and mix in the liquid to give a smooth batter. Whisk the egg whites until they form soft peaks and fold into the batter. Lightly oil a large waffle iron and place it on the hob for 1–2 minutes to heat. Spoon about a quarter of the mixture on to the iron and close it. Cook over a medium heat for about 2 minutes on each side, until crisp and golden. Take out and keep warm. Make 3–4 more waffles in the same way, then serve dusted with icing sugar.

APPLE PANCAKES

100g (3½oz) unsalted butter

2 eggs

250ml (8fl oz) milk

100g (3½oz) caster sugar

140g (4½oz) plain flour

pinch of salt

4 Golden Delicious apples, peeled, cored and cut in 6–8 rings each

icing sugar for dusting

TIP

Do not use cooking apples for this as they will fall apart. Cox's Orange Pippins, Granny Smith or Golden Delicious are ideal.

Melt 20g (¾oz) of the butter in a pan and heat it until it turns golden brown. Pass through a fine sieve. Whisk together the eggs, milk and 60g (2oz) of the sugar. Sift the flour and salt into a bowl, then whisk in the egg mixture and the browned butter until smooth.

In a large crêpe pan, melt a quarter of the remaining butter, add a quarter of the apple rings and sprinkle with a quarter of the remaining sugar. Cook for about 3 minutes on each side, until soft and caramelized. Pour a quarter of the batter over the apples and cook over a low heat for 2–3 minutes, until set. Slide on to a baking sheet, place the pan on top and invert the pancake back into the pan. Cook for 2 minutes, until golden brown. Slide on to a plate and keep warm. Make 3 more pancakes in the same way, then serve dusted with icing sugar.

DATE MOUSSE

200g (7oz) fresh dates, halved and stoned

2 tbsp dark rum

50g (1¾oz) icing sugar, sifted

450ml (¾ pint) double cream

3 egg whites

Rhubarb Compote (see page 36)

TIP

The cream should only be lightly whipped so it mixes better with the date purée.

An incredibly easy dessert, yet full of flavour. For a less sweet mousse, add lemon juice to taste to the date purée.

Planning ahead: The mousse and the compote can be prepared up to 1 day in advance.

In a liquidizer or food processor, purée the dates with the rum and half the icing sugar. Lightly whip the cream and fold the purée into it. Whisk the egg whites until stiff, then whisk in the remaining icing sugar a little at a time. Fold the egg whites into the date cream and chill. Serve with the rhubarb compote.

LEMON CRÈME BRÛLÉE WITH RASPBERRIES

500ml (16fl oz) double cream

2 vanilla pods, split

7 egg yolks

180g (6oz) caster sugar

juice of ½ lemon

finely grated zest of 2 lemons

100g (3½oz) raspberries

30g (1oz) icing sugar, sifted

The lemon really intensifies the flavour of the fruit and cream.

Planning ahead: The lemon cream can be prepared up to a day in advance and then caramelized shortly before serving. It should be eaten at room temperature rather than chilled.

Preheat the oven to 170°C/325°F/Gas Mark 3. Put the cream into a pan, scrape in the seeds from the vanilla pods and heat to simmering point. Beat the egg yolks with the caster sugar until pale, add the lemon juice and zest and stir in the cream. Place the raspberries in an ovenproof dish, pour the cream mixture over and bake in a bain-marie for about 30 minutes, until lightly set. Remove from the oven and leave until lukewarm. Sprinkle the icing sugar over the top and caramelize under a preheated grill set at maximum (better still, use a blow torch). Leave until the topping has cooled and hardened.

RHUBARB COMPOTE

200ml (7fl oz) orange juice

100ml (3½fl oz) white wine

100g (3½oz) caster sugar

1½ cinnamon sticks

pinch of ground ginger

400g (14oz) young rhubarb, cut into 10cm

(4 inch) pieces

Put all the ingredients except the rhubarb in a pan and simmer for 5 minutes. Add the rhubarb, cover and simmer until tender. Leave to cool.

WARM PEAR TART

350g (12oz) Sweet Pastry (see below)

500ml (16fl oz) sugar syrup (see page 109)

4 pears, peeled, halved and cored

400ml (14fl oz) double cream

½ vanilla pod, split

4 egg yolks

45g (1½oz) caster sugar

1–2 tbsp Poire William liqueur

TIP

Check the tart carefully after about 20 minutes, especially if you have an old oven with an uneven temperature. If necessary, turn the tart a couple of times to cook evenly. Do not overcook it under any circumstances.

Planning ahead: You can prepare the dough and line the tin the day before.

On a lightly floured surface, roll out the pastry thinly and use to line a 20cm (8 inch) spring-release cake tin so that the pastry comes 5cm (2 inch) up the sides of the tin. Line with greaseproof paper and fill with baking beans, then chill for at least 20 minutes while you preheat the oven to 190°C/375°F/Gas Mark 5. Bake the pastry case for 15 minutes, then remove the paper and baking beans and return to the oven for another 5–10 minutes, until lightly golden. Remove from the oven and reduce the temperature to 180°C/350°F/Gas Mark 4.

Heat the sugar syrup and poach the pear halves in it until just tender. Drain thoroughly and leave to cool. Put the cream in a pan, scrape the seeds from the vanilla pod into it and bring to boiling point. Remove from the heat and leave to infuse. Beat the egg yolks and sugar together until pale and then stir in the cream. Pass through a fine sieve and stir in the liqueur. Arrange the pear halves over the pastry case, pour the custard over and return to the oven for about 45 minutes, until set. Serve warm.

SWEET PASTRY

225g (8oz) unsalted butter

100g (3½oz) caster sugar

1 egg, beaten

350g (12oz) plain flour

salt

TIP

Divide the mixture into 3 batches – use one and freeze the other 2.

All the 20cm (8 inch) flans in this book require a third of this recipe. The pastry will keep for 3 days wrapped in the fridge.

Cream the butter and sugar together until very pale, then beat in the egg a little at a time. Gradually add the flour with a pinch of salt and mix to a smooth paste. Cover and leave to rest, ideally for 12–24 hours.

LUNCH

The frantic pace of modern life has led to many casualties, one of which is lunch. Enjoying a wholesome meal at lunchtime is a pleasure no one should give up without a fight! I firmly believe that we work harder, achieve more and feel better if a proper lunch is a routine part of our day.

Some lunches are an event in their own right. A Sunday roast, for example, is not something to be hurried. But time is not always on our side. Faced with a busy schedule, many people turn to 'convenience' food. This may be fast but it often contains an unhealthy mix of additives, chemicals and fat. There is, I am very glad to say, a middle path between fast food and complicated, time-consuming meals. The recipes in this chapter are for people who want to combine a good lunch with a busy life.

Taking lunch off the casualty list means following some basic rules. First and foremost – always keep it simple. A single main dish can be far more satisfying than a laboriously created three-course meal, so if you're short of time, just cook one course from the suggested menus in this section. Or try missing out the main course altogether and serving a starter followed by a dessert.

Keep to simple, high-quality ingredients. A few spears of fresh asparagus, the intense taste of thinly sliced Parma ham, the wonderful flavour of new potatoes – all these make for a healthy, refreshing lunch.

Even with simple dishes, preparation is important. A few minutes' planning the night before can save you valuable time in the morning.

Strike a blow for civilization! Join me in my campaign for lunches that make a landmark in the day.

LUNCH MENUS

EARLY SPRING MENU 40
Young Leek and Quails' Egg Salad
Braised Faggots and Goats' Cheese
  in Cabbage Leaves
Coffee-Flavoured Pot Crème with
  Almond and Orange Biscuits

SPRING MENU ONE 44
Sautéed Asparagus with Balsamic
  Vinegar and Parma Ham
Crisp Fried Lobster with Sesame
  Seed Dressing
Strawberry Punch with Lemon
    Sorbet

SPRING MENU TWO 47
Warm Salmon and Cucumber Salad
French Chicken Pithiviers with
  Lemon and Rosemary Cream
Old-fashioned Pancakes with
  Orange

SPRING MENU THREE 51
Linguine with Crab
Veal Kidneys in Lime Butter with
  Chicory
Fig Tart with Nuts and Ricotta

SUMMER MENU ONE 54
Provençal Vegetable Gratin
Baked Sea Bass Perfumed with
  Lemon Thyme
Filo Leaves with Summer Berries

SUMMER MENU TWO 58
Red Mullet Filled with Dill on
  Seasonal Leaves
Lamb Peperonata
Cherry and Almond Tart

SUMMER MENU THREE 61
Salad of Rocket with Feta, Lentils
  and Balsamic Onions
Tuna Steak Niçoise
Quark with Blueberries

SUMMER MENU FOUR 64
Chicken Tonnato with Beetroot
  Salad
Marinated Red Mullet and
  Sole
Exotic Summer Terrine

AUTUMN MENU ONE 67
Langoustines with Lentil and
  Smoked Bacon Ragout
Pigeon in a Salt Coat with Autumn
  Vegetables
Simple Apple Tarts with Cinnamon
  Cream

AUTUMN MENU TWO 71
Mangetout Salad with Lime Vinegar
  Dressing
Fillet of Grey Mullet on Julian's
  Ratatouille
Gooseberry Clafoutis

AUTUMN MENU THREE 74
Polenta and Gorgonzola on Greens
with Home-dried Tomatoes
Monkfish with Ginger and Saffron
  Basmati Rice
Chocolate and Chestnut Ice Cream

AUTUMN MENU FOUR 76
Clear Chilled Tomato Soup
Venison in Red Wine Pepper Sauce
  and Blueberries
Lemon Crêpe Gâteau

WINTER MENU ONE 79
Aubergine Gratin
Duck with Minted Tagliatelle
Meringue-glazed Apples in Caramel
  Sauce

NEW YEAR'S DAY MENU 83
Scallop and Potato Salad
Roast Pheasant with a Sour Shallot
  Sauce
Sticky Toffee Pudding

WINTER MENU TWO 86
Cream of Jerusalem Artichoke Soup
  with Watercress
Grilled Skirt Steak with Garlic and
  Chilli Dip
Chocolate and Nougat Pavé

EARLY SPRING MENU

YOUNG LEEK AND QUAILS' EGG SALAD
BRAISED FAGGOTS AND GOATS' CHEESE IN CABBAGE LEAVES
COFFEE-FLAVOURED POT CRÈME WITH ALMOND AND ORANGE BISCUITS

YOUNG LEEK AND QUAILS' EGG SALAD

20 quails' eggs

500g (1lb 1oz) baby leeks, trimmed and cut

on the diagonal into 5cm (2 inch) lengths

2 tbsp balsamic vinegar

4 plum tomatoes, blanched, peeled,

deseeded and cut into wedges

3 tbsp olive oil or basil oil

1 tbsp sherry vinegar

20g (¾oz) Parmesan cheese, cut into shavings

2 tbsp chopped chives

handful of rocket leaves

salt and peppermill

Leeks have a lot in common with onions but they are not as strong. They are very good flavour carriers and, of course, delightful vegetables in their own right.

Immerse the quails' eggs in boiling water for 1 minute, then drain and refresh in iced water. Carefully remove the shells.

Boil the leeks in plenty of salted water until tender but still firm, then drain and dry. Pour on the balsamic vinegar while the leeks are still warm, then add the tomato wedges.

Mix the oil with the sherry vinegar and season with salt and pepper. Pour half this dressing on to the eggs and warm them gently in a saucepan over the lowest possible heat.

Divide the leeks and tomatoes between 4 serving plates, top with the quails' eggs and sprinkle with the Parmesan cheese shavings and chives. Toss the rocket leaves in the remaining dressing, adjust the seasoning and place around the leeks.

TIP

Leeks are often grown on sandy soil so always wash them well in plenty of water.

YOUNG LEEK AND QUAILS' EGG SALAD

BRAISED FAGGOTS AND GOATS' CHEESE IN CABBAGE LEAVES

8 large Savoy cabbage leaves

1 onion, peeled and finely chopped

4 tbsp groundnut oil

2 cloves of garlic, peeled and crushed

4 tbsp milk

100g (3½oz) stale bread rolls or thinly sliced bread

150g (5oz) topside of beef

150g (5oz) shoulder of pork

2 eggs, beaten

4 tbsp double cream

2 sprigs of marjoram

100g (3½oz) firm goats' cheese, such as crottin de Chavignol or Roubiliac

500ml (16fl oz) chicken stock, warmed

chopped chives to garnish

salt and peppermill

This is very wholesome and warming, good for chilly early spring days. Whenever I make faggots or hamburgers I always use equal quantities of beef and pork plus some soaked bread. The pork provides moisture and flavour, while the goats' cheese adds its distinctive taste.

Blanch the cabbage leaves for 1 minute in boiling salted water, then drain and refresh in iced water. Cut out the stalks and dry the leaves on a clean tea towel. Season with salt and pepper.

Sweat the onion in the oil until translucent, then add the garlic. Sweat for a further minute and leave to cool.

Pour the cold milk on the bread and leave until it has been absorbed, then squeeze dry. Mince the beef, pork and bread through a fine mincer plate or in a food processor. Add the onion mixture, eggs and cream and stir in thoroughly.

Pick the marjoram leaves from the stalks, break the goats' cheese into even-sized pieces and add to the meat mixture. Season with salt and pepper. Divide the mixture into 8 portions, place each one on a cabbage leaf and fold in the sides, then roll up. Put them in a shallow flameproof casserole just large enough to hold them in a single layer and pour on the hot seasoned chicken stock. Bring to a simmer, then cover and cook for 15–20 minutes, until the faggots are firm to the touch. Remove the faggots from the casserole and keep warm. Boil the stock fast to reduce it by half its volume. Adjust the seasoning, then serve the faggots in soup plates with the stock. Garnish with chives.

TIP

Do not overseason the chicken stock or it will get too salty when you are reducing it.

COFFEE-FLAVOURED POT CRÈME WITH ALMOND AND ORANGE BISCUITS

250ml (8fl oz) milk

250ml (8fl oz) double cream

20g (¾oz) freshly ground coffee

5 egg yolks

75g (2½oz) caster sugar

For the biscuits

50g (1¾oz) unsalted butter, softened

finely grated zest of 1 orange

50g (1¾oz) icing sugar, sifted

1 tbsp plain flour

50g (1¾oz) nibbed almonds

Simple things in life often bring more joy than the over-sophisticated, and this old classic is a good example. It is light in texture and full of coffee flavour, and the preparation of it is, as you might say, dead easy. The biscuits could also be used as a petit four with coffee or brunch.

Preheat the oven to 150°C/300°F/Gas Mark 2. Put the milk, cream and coffee in a pan and simmer for 2 minutes, then remove from the heat and leave to infuse for 5 minutes. Beat the egg yolks and sugar together until pale and thick, then pour the hot milk on to them, stirring constantly. Pass the mixture through a fine sieve and pour into 4 ramekin dishes. If any foam has developed on top, remove it with an absorbent kitchen cloth.

Cook in a bain-marie in the oven for 35 minutes, until set. Remove and leave to cool, then cover with cling film to prevent a skin forming and chill until ready to serve.

For the biscuits, heat the oven to 220°C/425°F/Gas Mark 7. Cream the butter with the orange zest and icing sugar. Add the flour and almonds and mix until evenly combined. Spread ½ tablespoon quantities of the mixture into 5cm (2 inch) circles on baking trays lined with baking parchment. Bake for 4–5 minutes, until golden. Allow to cool slightly, then remove each biscuit from the baking parchment with a spatula and curve over a rolling pin for a few minutes until cold.

Serve the puddings with the almond and orange biscuits.

TIP

These biscuits are very delicate so handle with care. If they become too crisp to shape over the rolling pin, put them back in the oven for a few seconds to warm and soften.

SPRING MENU ONE

SAUTÉED ASPARAGUS WITH BALSAMIC VINEGAR AND PARMA HAM
CRISP FRIED LOBSTER WITH SESAME SEED DRESSING
STRAWBERRY PUNCH WITH LEMON SORBET

SAUTÉED ASPARAGUS WITH BALSAMIC VINEGAR AND PARMA HAM

28 green asparagus spears
2 tbsp groundnut oil
pinch of sugar
1 sprig of lemon thyme
8 slices of Parma ham
2 tsp balsamic vinegar
salt and peppermill

TIPS

Select medium to small size spears since these are much superior to the large ones. Check the head and the leaves for freshness; they should be moist and deep in colour. The bottom of each stem should snap off cleanly and be juicy. You can recognise if they are old, as they look tired.

As with so many other foods, the best way to prepare asparagus is to do as little as possible to it, so as not to lose its unique flavour, colour and character. If you are eating boiled asparagus, cook it immediately after peeling and refresh it in iced water to retain its colour. Green asparagus should always be cooked just enough to be slightly crunchy.

Asparagus should only be eaten during its season! Avoid asparagus out of season since, as with most other foods out of season, it comes from far corners of the world and is often 'tired' before it arrives here. Asparagus has a very distinctive and lovely flavour; it is also a good cleaning agent for your kidneys. Nowadays, there is also white asparagus from the continent, which are forced in sandbanks and dug out before their heads see the light of day; that is why they stay white. The white asparagus should be well peeled and then cooked in salted water with a little sugar, until they are well done. They have a good strong flavour, yet are more bitter than the local asparagus.

The best of all is, however, wild asparagus! You can find it sometimes in France, and it is apparently very common in Russia where the cows eat it. Wild asparagus is slightly purple in colour and has, like all asparagus, a very delicate flavour. If on your travels you come across it, it is an absolute 'must' – an experience you will remember all your life.

Asparagus is, without doubt, the 'King' of vegetables.

Planning ahead: Asparagus can be peeled a few hours in advance.

Heat the oven to 200°C/400°F/Gas Mark 6. Peel the asparagus, trim the stalk ends, then wash and dry on a kitchen cloth. In an ovenproof frying pan or a small roasting tin, sauté the asparagus in three-quarters of the groundnut oil for 1–2 minutes. Sprinkle with the sugar, remove the thyme leaves from the stalk and sprinkle them over the asparagus. Transfer to the oven and bake for about 10 minutes, turning the asparagus once. Season with salt and pepper and divide between 4 warmed plates.

Heat the remaining oil in a non-stick pan. Quickly fry the Parma ham for 2 seconds on each side, then add ½ teaspoon of the balsamic vinegar, turn the ham once more and place on the plates with the asparagus. Drizzle the remaining vinegar over.

CRISP FRIED LOBSTER WITH SESAME SEED DRESSING

4 x 750g (1½lb) live lobsters

1 large carrot, peeled

1 large courgette

Tempura Batter (see page 20)

8 large basil leaves

1 tsp sesame seeds, toasted

oil for deep frying

For the dressing

1 shallot, peeled and finely chopped

½ tsp freshly grated ginger

½ clove of garlic, peeled and crushed

½ red chilli, deseeded and chopped

4 tbsp soy sauce

½ tsp sugar

4 tbsp white wine vinegar

8 tbsp sesame oil

salt and peppermill

TIP

You can use tempura for all kinds of small pieces of food such as fish, vegetables and large herb leaves such as basil and the tops of celery. When fried, they are very pretty for garnishing food.

Lobster is highly prized for its unique flavour and texture. It has the highest meat yield of any crustacean and is relatively uncomplicated to prepare. The Scottish lobster is said to be more delicate than the American, which is reflected in its price.

Planning ahead: The lobster can be cooked the day before, in which case remove the shells, and wrap the meat in cling film.

Bring a large stockpot of salted water to the boil, then plunge one lobster into it and bring back to the boil. Cover and simmer for 5 minutes. Remove the lobster from the water and transfer to a large bowl of iced water. Cook the other 3 lobsters in the same way and refresh in iced water.

Take off the tail of each lobster and remove it from its shell. Take off the claws and divide them at their joints, then crack the shells to remove the white pieces of flesh. Cut the tail meat in 1cm (⅛ inch) slices and dry on a kitchen cloth. Cover and keep in a cool place.

Mix together all the ingredients for the dressing and set aside. Using a vegetable peeler, pare 'ribbons' from the carrot and courgette. Blanch in boiling salted water, then drain and refresh in iced water. Dry on a kitchen cloth.

Heat the oil to 180°C/350°F. Dip the lobster pieces in the tempura batter and fry in batches for about 2 minutes, until golden brown. Drain on kitchen paper and keep warm while you fry the rest. Dip the basil leaves in the last of the batter and briefly deep fry these as well.

Gently heat half the dressing in a pan and warm the vegetable ribbons in it. Arrange them on 4 serving plates. Top with the lobster and garnish with the basil leaves. Sprinkle with the toasted sesame seeds and serve with the remaining dressing.

STRAWBERRY PUNCH WITH LEMON SORBET

150ml (¼ pint) water

100g (3½oz) caster sugar

1 orange

1 gelatine leaf

450g (1lb) strawberries, hulled, cut into
quarters if large

100ml (3½fl oz) sparkling wine

4 sprigs of mint

For the lemon sorbet

1 gelatine leaf

150ml (¼ pint) water

150g (5oz) caster sugar

3 lemons

You can substitute any soft fruit in season for the strawberries. If you are feeling rich, try using champagne instead of sparkling wine.

Planning ahead: If you do not have an ice-cream machine, prepare the sorbet a day in advance.

For the punch, bring the water and sugar to boiling point, then remove from the heat. Cut the orange in half and add to the sugar syrup. Soak the gelatine leaf in water to cover for 10 minutes, then squeeze out the excess liquid and stir the gelatine into the sugar syrup. Leave to cool.

For the sorbet, soak the gelatine in water to cover, for 10 minutes. Put the measured water and sugar in a pan and heat until the sugar has dissolved completely. Squeeze the gelatine to remove excess liquid and stir it into the sugar syrup. Finely grate the zest of half a lemon into it. Squeeze the juice from all the lemons and add to the syrup. Freeze in an ice-cream machine according to the manufacturer's instructions. Alternatively, pour the mixture into a freezerproof container, cover and freeze until almost firm. Transfer to a food processor and whizz until broken up and well mixed. Return to the container and freeze again. For a finer-textured sorbet, repeat this process once more.

Just before serving, mix the sorbet well with a fork and, if it is too hard, place it in the fridge for 10–15 minutes.

To serve, place the strawberries in 4 shallow soup plates. Remove the orange halves from the punch and squeeze the juice back into it through a fine sieve. Stir in the sparkling wine and pour the punch carefully over the strawberries. With 2 serving spoons, shape the sorbet into quenelles and arrange one on top of each plate of strawberries. Decorate each portion with a sprig of mint.

SPRING MENU TWO

WARM SALMON AND CUCUMBER SALAD
FRENCH CHICKEN PITHIVIERS WITH LEMON AND ROSEMARY CREAM
OLD-FASHIONED PANCAKES WITH ORANGE

WARM SALMON AND CUCUMBER SALAD

2 large cucumbers, peeled and very thinly
sliced

2 tbsp white wine vinegar

3 tbsp olive oil

4 tbsp water

juice of 1 lemon

2 tsp caster sugar

½ tsp grated horseradish

2 tbsp chopped dill

350g (12oz) salmon fillet, skin, bones and fat
removed by your fishmonger

½ tbsp groundnut oil

1 tbsp sherry vinegar

4 small handfuls of small seasonal salad leaves

4 sprigs of dill to garnish

salt and peppermill

Wild salmon is obviously best but farmed will do quite nicely. The important thing here is that it should be extremely fresh.

Blanch the cucumber slices in boiling salted water for 5 seconds, then drain and refresh in iced water. Drain again and dry thoroughly. Make a marinade by mixing together the vinegar, 1 tablespoon of the olive oil, the water, half the lemon juice, plus the sugar, horseradish and salt and pepper to taste. Add the chopped dill and cucumber to the marinade and adjust the seasoning.

Wash the salmon fillet, dry well and cut it into 12 slices. Season with salt and pepper and the remaining lemon juice. Pour the groundnut oil into a shallow ovenproof dish, place the salmon pieces in it and cover with cling film. Heat in the oven on the lowest possible setting for about 5 minutes. The salmon should be just warmed through but not completely cooked; ideally it should still be translucent.

Mix together the sherry vinegar and the remaining olive oil with a little salt and pepper to make a dressing. Drain the cucumber and set a portion in the centre of each plate. Arrange the salmon slices on top. Toss the salad leaves in the dressing and arrange around the salmon, then garnish with the sprigs of dill.

FRENCH CHICKEN PITHIVIERS WITH LEMON AND ROSEMARY CREAM

60g (2oz) smoked back bacon, cut into strips

2 tbsp chopped shallots

15g (½oz) unsalted butter

1 tbsp groundnut oil

2 cloves of garlic, peeled and crushed

15g (½oz) bunch of mint, stalks removed,
leaves chopped

400g (14oz) skinless, boneless chicken breasts,
cut into 1.5cm (½ inch) cubes

400g (14oz) potatoes, peeled, very thinly
sliced, then blanched and dried

500g (1lb 1oz) puff pastry

1 egg yolk, beaten

400ml (14fl oz) double cream

200ml (7fl oz) dry white wine

6 Pan-fried Garlic Cloves (see page 23)

3 sprigs of rosemary

juice of ½ lemon

salt and peppermill

Rosemary, which grows wild, has a very intense flavour. It is mostly used to infuse fish, lamb and chicken and it also goes well with fried potatoes.

Planning ahead: Prepare the filling and place in puff pastry up to 4 hours in advance.

Blanch the bacon strips in boiling water for 30 seconds, then drain, refresh in iced water and dry on a kitchen cloth. Sweat the shallots in the butter and oil until soft, add the crushed garlic and sweat for a further minute. Add the bacon and cook until slightly crispy. Set aside.

Mix the mint, chicken and potatoes together and season with salt and pepper. Stir in the bacon mixture.

Divide the puff pastry in half. On a lightly floured surface, roll out one piece thinly and cut it to a 25cm (10 inch) round. Roll the remaining piece of pastry and cut to a 28cm (11 inch) round. Place the smaller circle of pastry on a greased baking sheet and top with the chicken mixture, leaving a 2cm (¾ inch) border. Brush the border with a little beaten egg yolk and top with the larger piece of puff pastry. Press the edges together to seal, then knock them up with a small knife and crimp to give a decorative effect. Cut a 2cm (¾ inch) circle, or 'chimney' out of the centre of the pastry lid. With the back of a knife, score half-circles about 2cm (¾ inch) apart, starting just below the 'chimney' and radiating out towards the edge. Brush with the remaining beaten egg yolk and leave to rest in a cool place for about 15 minutes. Preheat the oven to 200°C/400°F/Gas Mark 6.

Bake the Pithiviers for 30 minutes. Put half the cream in a pan and bring it just to the boil, then season lightly and pour it into the pie through the hole in the centre. Bake for a further 15 minutes, then test with a skewer to see if the filling is tender. If not, cook for 15 minutes longer. Remove from the oven and leave to rest for 10 minutes.

Put the white wine in a pan and boil until reduced by two-thirds. Add the remaining cream, the roasted garlic cloves and the rosemary sprigs and simmer until the sauce has reduced and is thick enough to coat the back of a spoon. Remove the rosemary and liquidize the sauce, then reheat gently. Season with salt and pepper and stir in the lemon juice.

Cut the pie into slices and serve with the sauce. A crisp salad goes very well with this dish.

WARM SALMON AND CUCUMBER SALAD, FRENCH CHICKEN PITHIVIERS WITH LEMON AND ROSEMARY CREAM, AND OLD-FASHIONED PANCAKES WITH ORANGE

OLD-FASHIONED PANCAKES WITH ORANGE

100g (3½oz) plain flour, sifted

pinch of salt

2 eggs

140g (4½oz) caster sugar

300ml (½ pint) milk

45g (1½oz) butter

6 oranges

200ml (7fl oz) water

2 tsp cornflour

2 tbsp Grand Marnier

icing sugar for dusting

4 sprigs of mint

This is my version of that classic dessert, Crêpes Suzette, which is now enjoying something of a comeback.

Mix the flour and salt in a large bowl, then add the eggs, 4 tablespoons of the sugar and about a quarter of the milk and mix to a thick batter. Slowly add the rest of the milk to give a thin pouring batter. If there are any lumps in it, pass it through a fine sieve.

Melt the butter in a pan until it begins to foam and then whisk half of it into the batter. Leave to rest in a cool place for 15 minutes.

Meanwhile, pare the zest from one orange with a vegetable peeler and cut it into long, thin strips. Blanch and drain. To caramelize it, dissolve the remaining sugar in the water over a gentle heat and then bring to the boil. Add the orange zest and boil gently for about 10 minutes, until the liquid has reduced to a pale golden caramel. Add about 2 tablespoons of cold water to stop the cooking, then remove from the heat and leave to cool.

Remove all the skin and white pith from 2 of the oranges and cut out the segments from between the membranes. Do this over a bowl to catch the juice and squeeze out the juice from the membranes once you have removed all the segments. Squeeze the juice from the remaining 4 oranges and add to the juice from the segmented oranges.

Mix 1 tablespoon of the orange juice with the cornflour. Bring the remaining orange juice to the boil and stir in the cornflour mixture. Cook, stirring, for 1–2 minutes, until lightly thickened. Remove from the heat and stir in the Grand Marnier. If the oranges are tart, you can add a little sugar.

Preheat the oven to 200°C/400°F/Gas Mark 6. Heat a 15cm (6 inch) diameter non-stick omelette pan, brush with a little of the remaining melted butter, then ladle in enough batter to cover the base of the pan in a thin layer, tilting the pan so the batter spreads evenly. Cook for 30 seconds over a medium-high heat until browned, then turn over and cook for a further 30 seconds. Continue making them in this way until all the batter is used up. There should be 12 pancakes. Fold each pancake into quarters, place them on a baking sheet, drizzle with orange sauce and reheat in the oven for 5–10 minutes. Be careful they do not dry out at the edges. Warm the caramelized orange zest and remove from the sugar syrup.

Reheat the sauce and pour enough on to each serving plate to cover the base. Dust the pancakes generously with icing sugar and arrange 3 on each plate. Decorate with the orange segments, caramelized zest and mint.

TIP

Should you really want to impress, serve these pancakes with one or two scoops of mandarin or orange sorbet.

SPRING MENU THREE

LINGUINE WITH CRAB
VEAL KIDNEYS IN LIME BUTTER WITH CHICORY
FIG TART WITH NUTS AND RICOTTA

LINGUINE WITH CRAB

a medium-sized live crab, or 90g (3oz) white
and 50g (1¾oz) brown prepared crab meat

3 cloves of garlic, peeled and chopped

3 red chillies, chopped (leave the seeds in if
you prefer a hot flavour)

1 bunch of spring onions, cut into
julienne strips

4 tbsp virgin olive oil

200ml (7fl oz) dry white wine

300g (10oz) fresh linguine

3 tbsp chopped parsley

salt and peppermill

TIP

A useful trick is to add a spoonful of
chicken stock or pasta cooking water to
the pasta just before tossing it with the
sauce; this makes it very smooth.

Chillies belong to the capsicum family. They come in different shapes and sizes, dried or pickled, or even smoked, and their strength varies greatly so you have to be careful. When preparing chillies, do not touch your eyes, and wash your hands and utensils well after use.
Once you have experimented with chillies, you will find that, when used with care, they are a great and versatile spice that can be used in many different dishes.
The contrast between the heat of chillies and the sweetness of crab meat and olive oil makes a delicately rich combination. Linguine are very fine noodles and are available either fresh or dried. However, you can use any kind of pasta for this recipe. Serve with chilled Italian white wine.

If you are using a live crab, plunge it into a large saucepan of boiling salted water, bring back to the boil and cook for 5 minutes. Transfer to a bowl of iced water until cool enough to handle. Remove the meat from the shell and separate the white and brown meat.

Sweat the garlic, chillies and spring onions in the olive oil until softened. Add the brown crab meat and the white wine and simmer for about 10 minutes, until reduced to a sauce-like consistency. Meanwhile, cook the linguine in plenty of boiling salted water (you don't need to add oil; this is an old wives' tale and simply not necessary) for 2–3 minutes until *al dente*. Drain.

Toss the linguine with the crab sauce and the chopped parsley. Toss in the white crab meat at the last minute and adjust the seasoning to taste.

VEAL KIDNEYS IN LIME BUTTER WITH CHICORY

4 small heads of chicory
juice of 2 limes
2 veal kidneys, fat removed, cut into slices
1cm (⅓ inch) thick (ask your butcher
to do this)
3 tbsp groundnut oil
1 tsp caster sugar
300ml (½ pint) medium sweet sherry
100g (3½oz) unsalted butter, chilled and cut
into cubes
salt and peppermill

Chicory is also known as Belgian endive and, to complicate matters further, it is sometimes confused with the lettuce known as curly endive or frisé. It has a very distinctive bitter flavour which brings out the best in the kidneys. It can be served raw in salads, fried or braised. You can also use the inner leaves to serve with dips. Or try using chicory with other meats such as chicken and beef.
Make sure that the veal kidneys are very fresh; they should be pink and moist.

Planning ahead: This dish has to be cooked at the last minute.

Remove any damaged outside leaves from the chicory heads, then cut them in half and remove any stalk and the central cores. Cut across into pieces 6mm (¼ inch) wide, wash well and dry. Toss with about a quarter of the lime juice.

Season the sliced kidneys and fry them quickly in 2 tablespoons of the oil for 2–3 minutes; they should still be pink in the centre. Remove and keep warm.

Pour away the fat from the pan, add the sugar and cook until caramelized, stirring continually. Be careful not to let it burn. Add the remaining lime juice and boil fast until reduced by two-thirds. Add the sherry and again reduce by two-thirds. Remove from the heat and whisk in the cold butter a little at a time. Season with salt and pepper and set aside; keep warm but do not boil.

Heat the remaining oil in a non-stick frying pan, and toss the chicory in it for 1–2 minutes to heat through. Season only with pepper. Arrange the chicory on a serving plate, top with the kidneys and serve the sauce on the side.

TIP
If the sauce separates while you are adding the butter, boil about 3 tablespoons of double cream until reduced, cool slightly, then whisk in 15g (½oz) cold butter pieces and very slowly whisk in the separated sauce.

FIG TART WITH NUTS AND RICOTTA

250g (8½oz) Sweet Pastry (see page 37)

6 dried figs, chopped

4 tbsp caster sugar

200ml (7fl oz) ruby port

200g (7oz) ricotta

30g (1oz) hazelnuts, finely chopped

60g (2oz) ground almonds

1 egg

finely grated zest of ½ lemon

pinch of freshly grated nutmeg

6–8 large fresh figs

For the streusel

75g (2½oz) plain flour

50g (1¾oz) caster sugar

1 tsp ground allspice

50g (1¾oz) unsalted butter, chilled and cut into small cubes

Make sure that you try a fig before purchasing them as they are often not sweet and ripe enough. You should eat them as soon as possible after purchasing because they lose their flavour and texture very quickly. Figs are very versatile; they are delicious eaten fresh but are also great when cooked. They go well with ham and poultry, especially duck, and are good in stews and desserts, too.

Roll out the pastry on a lightly floured surface and use to line a deep 20cm (8 inch) flan tin. Line the pastry case with greaseproof paper or kitchen foil and weight it down with baking beans. Rest it in a cool place for 20 minutes. Preheat the oven to 190°C/375°F/Gas Mark 5. Bake the pastry case for approximately 20 minutes, then remove the paper and beans and bake for a further 10 minutes until it is golden brown.

Meanwhile, put the dried figs in a small saucepan with half the sugar and the port and simmer for about 5 minutes until the port is slightly syrupy. Leave to cool.

Mix the ricotta, hazelnuts, ground almonds, egg, lemon zest, nutmeg and the remaining sugar together and spread over the pastry base. Cut each fresh fig in 4 thick slices and arrange on top of the ricotta mixture, overlapping them slightly.

For the streusel, combine the flour, sugar and allspice in a bowl. Rub in the butter until it forms large pea-sized crumbs. Sprinkle this mixture over the figs and bake in the oven for about 15 minutes, until the figs are slightly browned. Leave to cool and remove from the tin. Serve with the dried figs in port.

TIP

For a crisper streusel, sprinkle half on the tart and half on a baking sheet. Cook as above and, when the tart is cool, sprinkle the extra streusel mixture on top.

SUMMER MENU ONE

PROVENÇAL VEGETABLE GRATIN
BAKED SEA BASS PERFUMED WITH LEMON THYME
FILO LEAVES WITH SUMMER BERRIES

PROVENÇAL VEGETABLE GRATIN

1 medium aubergine, cut in half lengthways,
then into 6mm (¼ inch) slices
100ml (3½fl oz) olive oil
2 fennel bulbs, trimmed, cut into quarters
and thinly sliced
3 leeks, white part only, cut in half
lengthways and thinly sliced
2 onions, peeled and chopped
3 cloves of garlic, peeled and crushed
2 sprigs of thyme
2 medium courgettes, cut into
6mm (¼ inch) slices
3 plum tomatoes, blanched, peeled and cut
into 6mm (¼ inch) slices
15g (½oz) bunch of basil, stalks removed,
leaves shredded
60g (2oz) Parmesan cheese, freshly grated
salt and peppermill

Season the aubergine with salt and pepper and leave in a cool place for 20 minutes. Preheat the oven to 180°C/350°F/Gas Mark 4.

Heat 2 tablespoons of the oil in a heavy-based pan and add the fennel. Cook, stirring frequently, until almost soft. Add the leeks, season, then cover and cook until soft but not coloured. In another heavy-based pan, sweat the onions in 2 tablespoons of the oil until translucent, then add the garlic and sweat for a further minute. Add to the fennel mixture with the thyme and leave to infuse for a few minutes. Adjust the seasoning.

Squeeze excess liquid out of the aubergines. Heat the remaining oil in a large frying pan and fry the aubergines until slightly softened. Add the courgettes and fry for a few minutes longer, then adjust the seasoning.

Place the fennel and leek mixture in a 5cm (2 inch) deep ovenproof dish. It should come about half way up the sides. Layer the aubergines, courgettes and tomatoes on top and bake in the oven for 20 minutes.

Sprinkle the basil on top of the vegetables, then cover with the Parmesan cheese. Return to the oven for 10 minutes or place under a preheated grill to brown.

BAKED SEA BASS PERFUMED WITH LEMON THYME

4 x 350–400g (12–14oz) baby sea
bass (see method)
juice of 2 lemons
1 bunch of lemon thyme
100ml (3½fl oz) olive oil
12 small new potatoes
1 clove of garlic, peeled
knob of unsalted butter
salt and peppermill

TIPS
You could substitute red mullet or trout
for the sea bass.

Correct cooking time, as with all fish, is of
the essence.

Sea bass has become the fashionable fish of the Nineties and a premium has to be paid for it. I think it is well worth the money. Its flesh is firm and if you bake it, as in this recipe, you really bring out the best in it.

Planning ahead: Prepare everything in advance; the actual cooking time is then very short.

Ask your fishmonger to clean the fish, remove the scales and fins and criss-cross the skin on both sides.

Wash and dry the fish, season with salt and pepper and squeeze a little lemon juice inside and out. Stuff a generous sprig of lemon thyme into each belly cavity (you need to reserve 4 sprigs for garnish and 1 for the potatoes). Set the fish in a large dish and pour half the olive oil over them. Leave to marinate in the fridge for about 30 minutes. Meanwhile, heat the oven to 200°C/400°F/Gas Mark 6. Scrape the potatoes well and cut them into slices 3mm (⅛ inch) thick. Wash and dry the slices on a clean tea towel.

Remove the fish from the oil, place on a baking sheet and cook in the oven for 12–15 minutes. Heat the remaining oil in a non-stick frying pan and add the whole garlic clove and the potatoes. Season with salt and pepper and fry the potatoes gently on both sides for about 10 minutes, until lightly coloured and tender. Add the butter and a sprig of thyme and cook for a further minute. Remove the garlic.

Check the fish along the backbone with a small knife to see if they are cooked. The flesh should be white and come away easily from the bone. Place a sprig of thyme in the fin of each fish to garnish. Serve with the potatoes and a green salad.

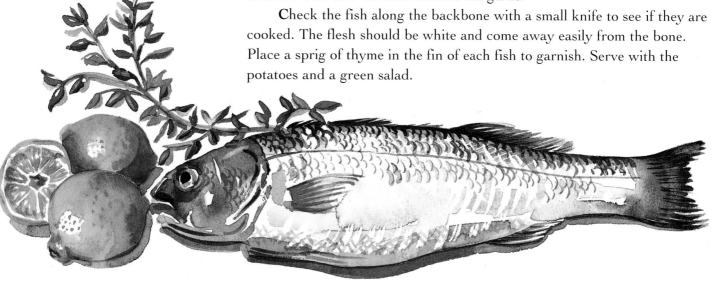

FILO LEAVES WITH SUMMER BERRIES

FILO LEAVES WITH SUMMER BERRIES

12 circles of filo pastry, 10cm (4 inch) in
diameter
100ml (3½fl oz) double cream
7 tsp icing sugar
100ml (3½fl oz) Greek yoghurt
200g (7oz) mixed fresh summer berries, such
as raspberries, blueberries, strawberries, wild
strawberries, blackberries
extra berries (optional) and mint sprigs
to decorate
Strawberrry Coulis (see below)

This is a quick and easy version of the famous French millefeuille, which came to us courtesy of the *nouvelle cuisine* movement. Such dishes made a fantastic impact on young chefs like myself at the time. Ones that survived the test of time, such as this one, prove that not all that came under the banner of *nouvelle cuisine* was bad.

Planning ahead: The filo discs can be done 6 hours in advance, and the strawberry sauce can be made the day before.

Preheat the oven to 200°C/400°F/Gas Mark 6. Place the filo circles individually on greased baking sheets, brush lightly with water and bake for 10–15 minutes until they are golden and lightly puffed up. Leave to cool.

Whip the double cream with 6 teaspoons of the icing sugar until it forms soft peaks, then stir in the yoghurt. Slice or quarter any strawberries, then carefully fold all the berries into the cream mixture.

Place a filo disc on each serving plate and spoon a little of the fruit mixture on top. Cover with another filo disc, add more fruit and top with a third filo disc. Repeat to make 3 more desserts in the same way, then dust the tops with the remaining icing sugar. Decorate with extra berries, if wished, and a mint sprig and then pour a little coulis around each dessert. Serve at once.

TIP

You can also use exotic fruit in place of soft fruit, and of course most fruit purées would be suitable as a sauce.

STRAWBERRY OR RASPBERRY COULIS

200g (7oz) strawberries, halved, or raspberries
45g (1½oz) icing sugar
1 tsp lemon juice

Place the strawberries or raspberries, icing sugar and lemon juice in a liquidizer, purée and then pass through a fine sieve.

SUMMER MENU TWO

RED MULLET FILLED WITH DILL ON SEASONAL LEAVES
LAMB PEPERONATA
CHERRY AND ALMOND TART

RED MULLET FILLED WITH DILL ON SEASONAL LEAVES

8 x 60g (2oz) red mullet fillets, scaled

5 tbsp olive oil

45g (1½oz) onion, peeled and finely chopped

1 clove of garlic, peeled and crushed

4 tbsp chopped dill

2 tbsp chopped parsley

30g (1oz) unsalted butter, softened

1 tbsp sherry vinegar

120g (4oz) mixed salad leaves

2 tbsp balsamic vinegar

salt and peppermill

A simple dish to prepare, yet quite original and full of the flavour of dill, which goes extremely well with the strong taste of the fish. Red mullet is available all year round and has firm flesh with a distinctive flavour. Dill has many other uses, in salads, soups and fish dishes, for example. In this country it is probably best known for pickling cucumbers. What a shame!

Planning ahead: You can prepare the dill filling a day in advance and fill the fish at the same time.

Preheat the oven to 200°C/400°F/Gas Mark 6. Wash the fish fillets well and dry them on a kitchen cloth. Use a pair of tweezers to remove as many small bones as possible from the fillets.

Heat 1 tablespoon of the olive oil in a pan, add the onion and sweat until translucent. Add the garlic and sweat for a further minute, then leave to cool. Transfer to a small bowl, add the chopped herbs and season with salt and pepper, then beat in the butter. Season the fish fillets with salt and pepper.

Divide the herb butter between 4 of the red mullet fillets, spreading it evenly over them right up to the edges. Top with the remaining 4 fillets, skin-side up, and press down firmly.

Heat a large non-stick frying pan, add 1 tablespoon of the remaining oil and cook the fillets quickly on both sides until coloured, turning them carefully. Transfer to a baking sheet and cook in the oven for about 5 minutes until just firm to the touch.

Mix together the sherry vinegar, remaining olive oil and salt and pepper to make a dressing. Toss the salad leaves in the dressing, arrange on plates and top with the red mullet. Sprinkle with the balsamic vinegar.

RED MULLET FILLED WITH DILL ON SEASONAL LEAVES

LAMB PEPERONATA

3 red peppers

3 yellow peppers

3 green peppers

1 aubergine

2 onions, peeled and finely chopped

200ml (7fl oz) extra virgin olive oil

2 cloves of garlic, peeled and finely chopped

3 plum tomatoes, blanched, peeled,
deseeded and diced

1 tbsp tomato purée

200ml (7fl oz) dry white wine

12 lamb cutlets

200ml (7fl oz) chicken or lamb stock

salt and peppermill

TIP

Instead of lamb cutlets, you could use
middle neck of lamb (ask your butcher to
cut it into pieces with the bones left on).

This traditional Italian dish is one of my favourites, as it is simple to prepare yet has a lot of flavour. It goes extremely well with a rocket salad.

Planning ahead: Like all other stews, it tastes better when it is reheated and therefore this can be prepared a day in advance.

Heat the oven to 190°C/375°F/Gas Mark 5. Grill the peppers until blackened and blistered on all sides. Transfer to a polythene bag and leave for 5 minutes or until cool enough to handle. Peel, deseed and cut into strips 1cm (⅓ inch) wide. Cut the aubergine lengthways into slices 1cm (⅓ inch), then cut into thin strips similar in size to the peppers.

Sweat the onions and aubergines in the olive oil in a large ovenproof casserole until soft. Add the garlic and sweat for a further minute. Add the tomatoes and cook for 3–4 minutes, then add the tomato purée and cook for 2–3 minutes. Add the wine and boil fast until it is reduced by half. Add the peppers and aubergines to the sauce and mix together, then add the lamb cutlets and cover with the pepper mixture. Pour in the stock and season generously. Bring back to a simmer, then transfer to the oven and cook, uncovered, for 45–60 minutes, stirring occasionally, until the meat is tender. Adjust seasoning and serve.

CHERRY AND ALMOND TART

250g (8½oz) Sweet Pastry (see page 37)

2 tbsp apricot jam

75g (2½oz) unsalted butter

75g (2½oz) caster sugar

1 egg

75g (2½oz) ground almonds

400g (14oz) jar of Griottines cherries in
Armagnac, or 425g (15oz) can of pitted
cherries, drained

icing sugar for dusting

Prepare the pastry a day in advance. Wrap in cling film and chill.

Preheat the oven to 190°C/375°F/Gas Mark 5. On a lightly floured surface, roll out the pastry about 3mm (⅛ inch) thick and use to line a deep 20cm (8 inch) flan tin. Spread the jam over the base of the pastry case. In a food processor, beat together the butter and sugar until light and fluffy. Add the egg and beat until well combined. Whizz in the almonds quickly and spoon the mixture into the pastry case, smoothing the surface.

Drain the cherries thoroughly and spread them out on kitchen paper for a minute or two to absorb excess liquid. Press them neatly into the paste and bake for about 45 minutes, until just set. The filling will puff up well. Dust with icing sugar and serve warm, with thick cream.

SUMMER MENU THREE

SALAD OF ROCKET WITH FETA, LENTILS AND BALSAMIC ONIONS
TUNA STEAK NIÇOISE
QUARK WITH BLUEBERRIES

SALAD OF ROCKET WITH FETA, LENTILS AND BALSAMIC ONIONS

20 button onions, peeled

4 tbsp extra virgin olive oil

100ml (3½fl oz) balsamic vinegar

100g (3½fl oz) Puy lentils

1–2 tbsp sherry vinegar, to taste

45g (1½oz) Home-dried Tomatoes in
Olive Oil (see page 30)

60g (2oz) rocket

30g (1oz) baby spinach

240g (8oz) feta cheese, cut into fairly
small cubes

small handful of flat-leaf parsley, chopped

salt and peppermill

Rocket is the most rediscovered salad leaf of this decade. It is slightly bitter in taste, very refreshing and goes well with balsamic vinegar and cheese. Better still is the wild rocket. However, if no rocket is available, use baby spinach instead.
Puy lentils from France are small and brown, with a delicate texture; unlike most varieties they do not become mushy when cooked.
Feta in my opinion is one of the most undervalued of cheeses.

Planning ahead: Prepare the onions a day in advance.

Pack the onions tightly into a small, heavy-based saucepan. Add 2 tablespoons of the olive oil and fry over fierce heat for about 5 minutes or until brown, turning them so that they colour evenly. Then reduce the heat, cover and cook for a further 5 minutes or until tender. Transfer the onions to a small bowl, pour on the balsamic vinegar and leave to marinate for 12 hours. They will keep in the fridge, covered, for 1–2 weeks and you can re-use the balsamic vinegar.

Wash the lentils well and then cook in plenty of salted water until they just have a bite, approximately 25 minutes. Drain, refresh in cold water and dry on a clean tea towel.

Mix the sherry vinegar with the remaining oil to make a dressing and season to taste. Mix the lentils with the dried tomatoes and three-quarters of the dressing. Adjust the seasoning and spoon them on to serving plates.

Toss the rocket, spinach and button onions in half the remaining dressing and arrange on top of the lentils. Place the feta cubes on top and sprinkle with the parsley. Pour the remaining dressing over the cheese.

TIP

The onions will keep for at least a week if refrigerated. They go well with many different dishes such as cold in salads, and hot with fish, meat and especially poultry.

Tuna Steak Niçoise

large pinch of saffron threads

150ml (¼ pint) hot water

12 small new potatoes

4 x 120g (4oz) tuna steaks

120ml (4fl oz) olive oil

1 tbsp white wine vinegar

a little lemon juice to taste

45g (1½oz) onion, peeled and finely chopped

150g (5oz) fine green beans, trimmed and blanched until al dente

4 anchovy fillets, chopped

12 black olives, stoned and roughly chopped

4 plum tomatoes, blanched, peeled, deseeded and diced

salt and peppermill

Fresh tuna is a tremendous fish and the Japanese have always been aware of this. They use it for making sushi, an intriguingly tasty morsel. When cooked medium rare, tuna is extremely juicy, with a texture not unlike beef.

Stir the saffron into the hot water and leave to cool. Put the potatoes in a pan, add the saffron liquid, then add enough cold water to cover. Bring to the boil and simmer until tender, then drain.

Meanwhile, brush the tuna steaks with 1 tablespoon of the olive oil and season with salt and pepper. Grill or fry for about 2 minutes on each side, depending on thickness, until medium rare in the centre, like steak. Keep warm.

Mix together the vinegar, remaining olive oil and a little lemon juice to taste, then season with salt and pepper. Add all the remaining ingredients except the tomatoes and warm gently in a saucepan. Adjust the seasoning and add the tomatoes. Divide most of the mixture between 4 plates, top with the warm tuna steaks and pour the remaining dressing on top. Serve with the saffron potatoes.

Quark with Blueberries

200g (7oz) quark cheese

4 egg whites

45g (1½oz) caster sugar

200ml (7fl oz) double cream

finely grated zest of 1 lemon

½ tbsp vanilla sugar

200g (7oz) blueberries

4 sprigs of mint

Strawberry Coulis (see page 57)

Quark was my mother's favourite shortcut to a pudding on a busy day. Of course, you can use any other soft summer fruit.

Planning ahead: This can be prepared 4 hours in advance. Just mix in the berries at the last minute before serving.

Wrap the quark in muslin, then squeeze it to remove excess liquid. Whisk the egg whites to stiff peaks, then whisk in the sugar a little at a time until the mixture is thick and glossy.

Whip the cream until it forms soft peaks, add the lemon zest and vanilla sugar, then fold into the quark. Next fold in the egg white mixture and stir in half the blueberries.

Spoon the quark mixture on to large serving plates and arrange the remaining blueberries on top. Decorate each one with a sprig of mint and pour the strawberry coulis around.

SALAD OF ROCKET WITH FETA, LENTILS AND BALSAMIC ONIONS,
TUNA STEAK NIÇOISE, AND QUARK WITH BLUEBERRIES

SUMMER MENU FOUR

CHICKEN TONNATO WITH BEETROOT SALAD
MARINATED RED MULLET AND SOLE
EXOTIC SUMMER TERRINE

CHICKEN TONNATO WITH BEETROOT SALAD

4 tbsp olive oil

½ small onion, peeled and finely chopped

2 cloves of garlic, crushed

50g (1¾oz) celery, finely diced

50g (1¾oz) carrots, finely chopped

2 plum tomatoes, cut into quarters

1 sprig of thyme

½ bay leaf

100ml (3½fl oz) dry white wine

4 skinless, boneless chicken breasts

150g (5oz) canned tuna fish in oil, drained

1 tbsp mayonnaise

100ml (3½fl oz) double cream

1 tsp lemon juice

100ml (3½fl oz) chicken stock

1 tbsp white wine vinegar

180g (6oz) cooked beetroot, thinly sliced

2 tbsp capers

salt and peppermill

Be sure to buy plain beetroot for this recipe, rather than the type that has been drenched in vinegar.

Planning ahead: You can prepare the sauce a day in advance. The sauce will thicken as it sits in the fridge overnight; thin it down with a little chicken stock or, if not available, add a little milk.

Heat the oven to 190°C/375°F/Gas Mark 5. Heat 2 tablespoons of the olive oil in a flameproof casserole and sweat the onion until translucent. Add the garlic and sweat for a further minute, then add the celery, carrots, tomatoes, thyme, bay leaf and white wine. Season with salt and pepper.

Season the chicken breasts and place them on top of the vegetables. Transfer to the oven and roast for 15–20 minutes, turning the chicken once, until cooked through. Remove the chicken and leave to cool; do not refrigerate.

Cover the vegetables with a lid and continue cooking for 20 minutes or until well done. Stir in the tuna and cool slightly, then process very finely in a food processor. Leave to cool, then stir in the mayonnaise, cream and lemon juice and adjust the seasoning to taste. Thin to a coating consistency with the chicken stock and pass through a fine sieve or a mouli to give a smooth sauce.

Thinly slice the tepid chicken breasts and arrange each one in a single layer on a serving plate. Spread the sauce thinly and evenly on top.

Mix the vinegar with the remaining olive oil and season with salt and pepper. Toss the beetroot in this dressing, adjust the seasoning and arrange around the chicken. Sprinkle with the capers.

TIP

This dish can also be made with veal.

MARINATED RED MULLET AND SOLE

4 tbsp balsamic vinegar

1 tbsp white wine vinegar

3 tbsp olive oil

4 x 60g (2 oz) red mullet fillets

4 x 60g (2 oz) sole fillets

1 carrot, peeled, finely sliced and blanched

60g (2oz) fine green beans, trimmed
and blanched

2 plum tomatoes, blanched, peeled,
deseeded and diced

4 sprigs of chervil

salt and peppermill

TIP

You can use any other fish for this recipe
and instead of steaming you can grill or
even fry the fish in a little olive oil.

This makes an exquisite summer dish.

Planning ahead: The fish can be steamed 20 minutes in advance and then placed in the cold dressing and gently reheated as you warm the dressing.

Mix half the balsamic vinegar with the white wine vinegar, olive oil, salt and pepper and heat gently in a wide pan. Season the fish fillets and steam for 3–4 minutes, until just cooked. Check by inserting a knife; the fish should be opaque. Place the fish in the warm dressing and let it infuse for a few minutes, then transfer to a serving dish. Add the carrot, green beans and tomatoes to the dressing, warm through gently and adjust the seasoning. Pour this over the fish, garnish with the chervil and sprinkle with the remaining balsamic vinegar.

EXOTIC SUMMER TERRINE

200ml (7fl oz) dry white wine

100g (3½oz) caster sugar

2 tbsp lemon juice

2 tbsp orange juice

5 ripe peaches or nectarines

6 gelatine leaves

1 tbsp chopped mint

100g (3½oz) strawberries, hulled and
cut in half

50g (1¾oz) raspberries

50g (1¾oz) blueberries

50g (1¾oz) blackberries

50g (1¾oz) seedless green grapes

Strawberry Coulis (see page 57)

Planning ahead: You can use any fruit in season for this terrine. It is best made a day in advance.

Put the white wine, sugar, lemon juice and orange juice in a pan and heat until the sugar dissolves. Cut 3 of the peaches or nectarines in half, remove the stones and simmer in the liquid until soft. Purée in a food processor with half the cooking liquor. Soak the gelatine leaves in cold water for about 10 minutes, until softened, then squeeze to remove excess liquid and add to the remaining warm liquor. Heat gently until the gelatine has dissolved. Add to the purée in the food processor and work until smooth. Then stir in the chopped mint (do not process).

Line a 1.5 litre (2½ pint) terrine mould with cling film and pour in enough purée just to cover the base. Chill in the fridge until set. Arrange the strawberries in a tightly packed layer on the purée, leaving a gap between the fruit and the edges of the terrine. Pour on a little more purée so the strawberries are just covered and then chill until set.

Once set, arrange a very closely packed layer of berries and grapes on top of the strawberries, cover with purée and chill until set. Thinly slice the remaining peaches or nectarines and make a final layer with them and the last of the purée.

Refrigerate the terrine overnight. Unmould it and use a very sharp knife to cut the terrine into slices about 1.5cm (½ inch) thick. Serve with the strawberry coulis.

AUTUMN MENU ONE

LANGOUSTINES WITH LENTIL AND SMOKED BACON RAGOUT
PIGEON IN A SALT COAT WITH AUTUMN VEGETABLES
SIMPLE APPLE TARTS WITH CINNAMON CREAM

LANGOUSTINES WITH LENTIL AND SMOKED BACON RAGOUT

12 button onions, peeled

3 tbsp groundnut oil

20g (¾oz) unsalted butter

100g (3½oz) onions, peeled and
finely chopped

2 cloves of garlic, peeled and chopped

50g (1¾oz) smoked bacon, cut into 6mm
(¼ inch) strips

½ tbsp tomato purée

100g (3½oz) Puy lentils, rinsed well

400ml (14fl oz) chicken or fish stock

12 live langoustines (Dublin Bay prawns)

chervil to garnish

salt and peppermill

The ragout can of course be used in many different dishes, especially with fried fish and pork.

Planning ahead: The beauty of this dish is that the Lentil Ragout can be made 1-2 days in advance and it tastes better after it is reheated.
The eventual preparation time can be as little as 2-3 minutes for frying the langoustines.

Place the button onions in a small, heavy-based pan with half the groundnut oil and fry for about 5 minutes, until they are an even brown colour. Season with salt and pepper, cover and cook over a very gentle heat for a further 5 minutes or until tender.

Meanwhile, melt the butter in a heavy-based pan, add the onions and cook without browning until soft. Add the garlic and cook for 2–3 minutes, then add the bacon and cook for a further 2 minutes. Stir in the tomato purée and cook for 2 minutes, then add the lentils and the stock. Bring to the boil, reduce the heat and simmer, covered, for 15 minutes, stirring occasionally. Add the cooked button onions and continue to cook for a few minutes or until the lentils are tender.

Drop the langoustines into a large saucepan of boiling water, then drain at once. Refresh in iced water and then peel them carefully to remove the tails. Dry on a kitchen cloth, season with salt and pepper and fry quickly in a hot pan with the remaining oil, turning them once, until they are pink and opaque. Spoon the lentil ragout into soup plates, arrange the langoustine tails on top and garnish with chervil.

TIP
Like most shellfish, langoustines are available all year round. The colder the water they live in, the better the texture and flavour. When buying them, always check that they are still alive.

PIGEON IN A SALT COAT WITH AUTUMN VEGETABLES

PIGEON IN A SALT COAT

4 squab pigeons, oven ready and trussed

4 tbsp groundnut oil

250g (8½oz) coarse sea salt

100g (3½oz) table salt

500g (1lb 1oz) plain flour

50g (1¾oz) cornflour

generous pinch of thyme leaves

2 egg whites

4 slices of bread, toasted

salt and peppermill

Cooking pigeon in a salt crust keeps in the flavour and when you remove the salt all the aromas are released.

Planning ahead: You can have the pigeon ready in the salt coat 4 hours in advance. The onion purée can be prepared in advance and it freezes well.

Season the pigeons with pepper and stuff the central cavity with crumpled silver foil so no salt can fall into it. Heat the oven to 220°C/425°F/Gas Mark 7.

Heat the oil in a pan until very hot and seal the pigeons on all sides, then leave to cool. Using your hands, mix both salts together with the flour, cornflour, thyme, egg whites and sufficient water to make a firm dough. Place each pigeon on a slice of toast and completely encase the bird in a layer of the salt mixture, pressing it on with your hands. Place in a roasting tin and cook in the oven for 45 minutes. Transfer the pigeons to a serving dish and remove the salt crust with a strong knife at the table.

AUTUMN VEGETABLES

12 chestnuts

30g (1oz) caster sugar

100ml (3½fl oz) dry white wine

1 tbsp plain flour

½ lemon

120g (4oz) salsify, peeled, cut into batons and kept in water acidulated with lemon juice

60g (2oz) Brussels sprouts, trimmed

60g (2oz) carrots, peeled and cut into batons

60g (2oz) courgettes, peeled and cut into batons

60g (2oz) swede, peeled and cut into batons

30g (1oz) unsalted butter

1 plum tomato, blanched, peeled, deseeded and finely diced

salt and peppermill

Cut a cross in the skin of each chestnut, place in a pan of cold water and bring to the boil. Remove the chestnuts and, when cool enough to handle, peel off both the outer and inner skins. Place the sugar and white wine in a small, heavy-based pan and cook over a medium heat for 2–3 minutes, until amber in colour. Add the chestnuts and cook until the sugar syrup is dark brown and coats the chestnuts – about 5 minutes. Remove from the heat.

Mix the flour to a paste with a little water, then stir it into 500ml (16fl oz) boiling salted water. Add the lemon half and salsify and boil for about 10 minutes, until tender. Leave the salsify to cool in the liquid, then remove and wash off the flour.

Boil all the other vegetables in plenty of salted water until *al dente*, then drain and refresh. Heat the butter in a pan, add the vegetables and a spoonful of water and cook until the water has evaporated and the butter coats the vegetables. Add the diced tomato and the chestnuts and adjust the seasoning.

SIMPLE APPLE TARTS WITH CINNAMON CREAM

300g (10oz) puff pastry

1 egg, beaten

100g (3½oz) caster sugar

300ml (½ pint) water

20g (¾oz) cinnamon sticks (about 8)

100ml (3½fl oz) crème fraîche

Frangipane (see below)

2 dessert apples, peeled, cored and thinly sliced

45g (1½oz) apricot jam, warmed and sieved

The best apples for this dish are Cox's Orange Pippin and Golden Delicious. The cinnamon brings a wonderful aroma to the apples.

Planning ahead: This can be made a few hours in advance and then reheated.

Roll out the puff pastry on a lightly floured surface until it is about 3mm (⅛ inch) thick and cut out four 12.5cm (5 inch) rounds. Re-roll the pastry trimmings and cut out strips 1cm (⅓ inch) wide. Brush the edges of the puff pastry rounds with the beaten egg and place the strips around the edge. Make cuts in the strips of puff pastry at 2.5cm (1 inch) intervals around the outside edge. Fold the right-hand outside corner of one cut over to the left-hand inside corner of the next cut to form a point and press firmly. Repeat until each pastry has a star-shaped edging. Leave to rest in the fridge for 20 minutes. Preheat the oven to 200°C/400°F/Gas Mark 6.

In the meantime, make the cinnamon cream, dissolve the sugar in the water with the cinnamon sticks, then cook until reduced to a very heavy syrup (about 100ml/3½fl oz). Leave to cool, then pass through a fine sieve and mix thoroughly with the crème fraîche.

Spread the frangipane in the middle of the star-shaped pastries and arrange the apple slices evenly on top. Bake the tarts for 20 minutes, until the pastry is golden brown and the apple tender. Remove from the oven and brush with the warmed apricot jam. Serve warm, with the cinnamon cream.

FRANGIPANE

30g (1oz) unsalted butter

30g (1oz) caster sugar

2 tbsp beaten egg

30g (1oz) ground almonds, sifted

1 tbsp plain flour, sifted

Cream the butter and sugar until pale, using a mixer set on high speed. Add the egg and beat slowly until well incorporated. Fold in the almonds and flour.

AUTUMN MENU TWO

MANGETOUT SALAD WITH LIME VINEGAR DRESSING
FILLET OF GREY MULLET ON JULIAN'S RATATOUILLE
GOOSEBERRY CLAFOUTIS

MANGETOUT SALAD WITH LIME VINEGAR DRESSING

juice of ½ lime

½ tbsp white wine vinegar

pinch of sugar

6 tbsp extra virgin olive oil or grapeseed oil

1 tbsp Dijon mustard

2 tbsp finely chopped shallots

½ tsp freshly grated ginger

200g (7oz) small mangetout

4 heads of chicory

1 tomato, blanched, peeled, deseeded
and diced

3 tbsp pine kernels

salt and peppermill

Planning ahead: Everything can be prepared up to 6 hours in advance. All you then have to do is toss the vegetables in the dressing and arrange on the plates.

Mix the lime juice, white wine vinegar, sugar, oil, mustard, shallots and ginger together and season well with salt and pepper.

Blanch the mangetout in boiling salted water for 15 seconds, then drain, refresh in iced water and dry with a clean tea towel.

Remove all the damaged outer leaves from the chicory and discard, then take off 28 medium-sized leaves, wash and reserve. Cut the remaining chicory in half and slice approximately 6mm (¼ inch) thick. Toss the large chicory leaves in some of the dressing and fan out on serving plates. Toss the chopped chicory, mangetout and diced tomato in the remaining dressing and adjust the seasoning. Arrange in the centre of the plates and sprinkle with the pine kernels.

MANGETOUT SALAD WITH LIME VINEGAR DRESSING, FILLET OF GREY MULLET ON JULIAN'S RATATOUILLE,
AND GOOSEBERRY CLAFOUTIS

FILLET OF GREY MULLET ON JULIAN'S RATATOUILLE

4 x 120g (4oz) grey mullet fillets

200ml (7fl oz) groundnut oil

6 spring onions, green part only, cut into
fine strips

2 sprigs of rosemary

For the ratatouille

100g (3½oz) onions, peeled and chopped

2 tbsp vegetable oil

15g (½oz) garlic cloves, peeled

100g (3½oz) red pepper, diced

100g (3½oz) yellow pepper, diced

100g (3½oz) green pepper, diced

100g (3½oz) courgettes, diced

15g (½oz) basil, stalks removed, leaves cut
into strips

100ml (3½fl oz) olive oil

30g (1oz) Parmesan cheese, freshly grated

salt and peppermill

TIP

This ratatouille also goes well with lamb.

Grey mullet is available all year round and is a rather neglected fish, which is a great shame as the flavour is not unlike sea bass and the flesh is soft. It is also a very good fish to bake with herbs.

Planning ahead: The ratatouille will last for 2 days in the fridge.

For the ratatouille, sweat the onions in the vegetable oil until translucent, add the garlic and sweat for a further minute. Add the peppers and courgettes and cook for about 15 minutes, without colouring, until tender. Liquidize to a rough purée.

Wash and dry the fish on a kitchen cloth. Use tweezers to remove all the little bones.

Heat 150ml (¼ pint) of the oil in a large saucepan to 130°C/260°F and fry the spring onions until crispy. Remove from the pan, drain on kitchen paper and keep warm.

Gently reheat the ratatouille, stir in the basil, olive oil and Parmesan cheese and season to taste.

Season the fish with salt and pepper. Heat the rest of the groundnut oil in a non-stick frying pan, put in the fish fillets, skin-side down, and the rosemary and fry for 2–3 minutes, until the skin is very crispy. Turn over and fry a little longer in order that the rosemary can infuse the fish, but be careful not to overcook it.

Place a generous amount of ratatouille purée on each serving plate and top with the fish, then place a generous heap of spring onions on top.

GOOSEBERRY CLAFOUTIS

3 eggs

75g (2½oz) caster sugar

75g (2½oz) ground almonds

45g (1½oz) unsalted butter, melted

6 tbsp double cream

1 tbsp brandy

120g (4oz) gooseberries

icing sugar for dusting

Preheat the oven to 180°C/350°F/Gas Mark 4. Grease and flour a 20cm (8 inch) cake tin and line with baking parchment, or use an ovenproof dish. Beat the eggs and sugar together, then stir in the ground almonds. Whisk in the melted butter, cream and brandy. Pour the mixture into the prepared tin and arrange the gooseberries on top, then bake for about 40 minutes, until set and golden.

Cool for 15 minutes, then dust with icing sugar.

AUTUMN MENU THREE

POLENTA AND GORGONZOLA ON GREENS WITH HOME-DRIED TOMATOES
MONKFISH WITH GINGER AND SAFFRON BASMATI RICE
CHOCOLATE AND CHESTNUT ICE CREAM

POLENTA AND GORGONZOLA ON GREENS WITH HOME-DRIED TOMATOES

1 onion, peeled and chopped

120ml (4fl oz) olive oil

2 small cloves of garlic, peeled and crushed

½ tsp lemon juice

500ml (16fl oz) chicken stock

90g (3oz) polenta

pinch of ground allspice

45g (1½oz) Parmesan cheese, freshly grated

2 tbsp sherry vinegar

2 tsp Acacia honey

½ tsp Worcestershire sauce

½ tsp Dijon mustard

140g (4½oz) baby spinach

100g (3½oz) Gorgonzola cheese, cut
into 4 slices

45g (1½oz) Home-dried Tomatoes in
Olive Oil (see page 30)

salt and peppermill

Polenta is a great carrier for strong flavours or sauces.

Place the onion and 4 tablespoons of the olive oil in a heavy-based pan and cook gently until the onion is soft. Add the garlic, turn up the heat and cook until the onion and garlic are slightly browned. Reduce the heat, cover and cook slowly for 20 minutes, stirring frequently. Leave to cool, then add the lemon juice and purée in a food processor until smooth.

Bring the chicken stock to the boil with a large pinch of salt and add the polenta all at once, stirring constantly. Stir in the allspice and cook over a gentle heat, stirring frequently, for 20 minutes, then add the Parmesan cheese.

Gently reheat the onion purée. Mix together the sherry vinegar, honey, Worcestershire sauce, mustard, remaining olive oil and salt and pepper to make a dressing. Toss the spinach with a little dressing. Place a spoonful of polenta on each plate and top with the onion mixture, then add a slice of Gorgonzola. Arrange the spinach around it and garnish with dried tomatoes.

TIPS

The onion purée will keep in the fridge
for 2–3 weeks.

If you use instant polenta it will take only
3–5 minutes to cook.

MONKFISH WITH GINGER AND SAFFRON BASMATI RICE

500g (1lb 1oz) monkfish fillets, all skin
removed (ask your fishmonger to do this)

½ tsp garam masala

2 tbsp light soy sauce

4 tbsp dry sherry

1 tbsp freshly grated ginger

300g (10oz) basmati rice

900ml (1½ pints) chicken stock

pinch of saffron threads

4 tbsp olive oil

1 tsp lemon juice

200ml (7fl oz) dry white wine

2 cloves of garlic, peeled and cut into paper-
thin slices

1 tsp chopped tarragon

salt and peppermill

Basmati rice should always be cooked in chicken stock rather than water.

Dry the fish on a kitchen cloth and cut it into 2cm (¾ inch) pieces. Mix together the garam masala, soy sauce, sherry and ginger and marinate the fish in this mixture for 10 minutes.

Put the rice in a deep pan, cover with plenty of water and bring to the boil. As it comes to the boil, drain through a sieve and then return the rice to the pan. Add the chicken stock, plus a little salt and the saffron. Simmer gently until the chicken stock has been absorbed and the rice is tender – about 5–7 minutes. In the meantime, drain the fish, reserving the marinade. Heat a heavy-based pan, add the oil and cook the fish over a high heat for 1–2 minutes, until coloured on all sides. Remove from the pan.

Add the marinade, lemon juice and wine to the pan and boil fast to reduce by half. Return the fish to the pan and cook over a high heat for 4–5 minutes until the fish is cooked through and the liquid reduced to a thick glaze. Add the garlic, simmer for another 30 seconds and remove from the heat. Stir in the tarragon and adjust the seasoning. Serve with the rice.

CHOCOLATE AND CHESTNUT ICE CREAM

250ml (8fl oz) milk

250ml (8fl oz) double cream

30g (1oz) cocoa powder, sifted

60g (2oz) Acacia honey

7 egg yolks

90g (3oz) caster sugar

30g (1oz) good-quality plain chocolate, finely
chopped

75g (2½oz) marrons glacés, chopped

Raspberry Coulis (see page 57)

Bring the milk, cream, cocoa powder and honey to the boil in a heavy-based pan. Beat the egg yolks with the sugar until thick and pale. Pour the hot milk mixture on to the yolks, stirring all the time. Wash the pan and pour the egg mixture back into it, then cook over a very gentle heat, stirring constantly, until the custard is thick enough to coat the back of the spoon. Do not let it boil.

Remove from the heat and whisk in the chocolate. Pass through a fine sieve, then leave to cool. Mix in the marrons glacés. Freeze in an ice-cream machine according to the manufacturer's instructions. Alternatively, pour the mixture into a large freezerproof bowl; do not add the marrons glacés. Cover and freeze until almost set. Transfer to a food processor and whisk until it is creamy and all the ice crystals have broken down. Put the mixture back in the bowl, cover and return to the freezer. Repeat this process twice, then stir in the marrons glacés and the ice cream is ready. Serve with the raspberry coulis.

AUTUMN MENU FOUR

CLEAR CHILLED TOMATO SOUP
VENISON IN RED WINE PEPPER SAUCE AND BLUEBERRIES
LEMON CRÊPE GÂTEAU

CLEAR CHILLED TOMATO SOUP

1 red pepper

1 kg (2¼lb) sweet, ripe tomatoes

3 cloves of garlic, peeled and crushed

2 sprigs of mint

4 gelatine leaves

salt and peppermill

To enjoy the full flavour of this soup you need to find tomatoes that are sun-ripened and sweet.

Planning ahead: This soup has to be prepared a day in advance. It freezes very well. However, if freezing it add the gelatine once it has defrosted.

Cut the pepper in half, remove the seeds and pith, then place under a hot grill and cook until the skin is blackened and blistered. Put the pepper in a bag and leave for 5 minutes (this makes the skin easier to remove). Peel off the skin. Roughly chop the pepper and tomatoes and place in a food processor with the garlic and mint. Whizz to a fine purée.

Transfer the mixture to a muslin-lined sieve set over a bowl and leave to drip for 8 hours in the fridge. Squeeze out all the liquid from the muslin and discard the pulp.

Soak the gelatine in water to cover for 10 minutes, then squeeze out excess liquid. Warm a small amount of the soup and add the gelatine to it. When it has completely dissolved, stir in the rest of the soup and adjust the seasoning to taste. Chill in the fridge until it is just setting – about 1–2 hours (you can prepare the soup well in advance and leave it in the fridge until ready to serve).

TIP

If you are cooking a dish that will later be served cold, remember to add plenty of seasoning and to taste it again before serving, because chilling blunts the flavours. It is sometimes wise to cool down a small quantity quickly in the freezer or on ice, so you can check precisely what it tastes like.

VENISON IN RED WINE PEPPER SAUCE AND BLUEBERRIES

4 tbsp groundnut oil

200g (7oz) venison bones and trimmings

1 onion, peeled and chopped

1 carrot, peeled and chopped

½ leek, chopped

2 celery sticks, chopped

½ tbsp tomato purée

100ml (3½fl oz) red wine

800ml (1 pint 7fl oz) chicken stock

½ tbsp black peppercorns

a few sprigs of thyme

450g (1lb) chestnuts

200g (7oz) celeriac, peeled and diced

4 tbsp double cream

1 pear, peeled, quartered and cored

2 tbsp caster sugar

1 cinnamon stick

4 x 150g (5oz) pieces of venison fillet (from
the eye of the loin)

1 tbsp red wine vinegar

1 tbsp redcurrant jelly

90g (3oz) blueberries

sprigs of mint

salt and peppermill

TIP

You can also trim and cut the meat and
then marinate it in oil, herbs and garlic. It
will keep for 2 weeks in the fridge.

Good quality venison – especially the farmed variety – has become readily available in supermarkets, and in my opinion, if you choose the fillet of the saddle it can hold its own very well with many other fillets such as beef or lamb. The flavour is clean, deep and elegant and it lends itself to many different ways of cooking. However, like all game do not overcook it as it will become dry.

Preheat the oven to maximum. Heat 2 tablespoons of the oil in a roasting tin on the hob and brown the bones and trimmings well on all sides. Transfer to the oven and roast for 15 minutes. Add the chopped vegetables and tomato purée and roast for a further 10 minutes. Remove from the oven and reduce the temperature to 200°C/400°F/Gas Mark 6.

Add the red wine, 500ml (16fl oz) of the stock and the peppercorns and thyme to the meat trimmings and simmer on the hob for 20 minutes. Pass through a fine sieve into a clean saucepan and boil until reduced to 300ml (½ pint). Reserve for the sauce.

Cut a cross in the skin of each chestnut, place in a pan of cold water and bring to the boil. Remove the chestnuts one at a time and peel off both the outer and inner skins. Cook the chestnuts and celeriac in the remaining stock with salt and pepper until tender, then drain. Boil the liquid fast to reduce it by half, then combine with the chestnuts and celeriac and purée in a food processor. Stir in the cream and adjust the seasoning.

Put the pear quarters in a pan with water just to cover, add the sugar and cinnamon stick and poach until tender but still firm.

Remove all the skin and sinew from the venison and season with salt and pepper. Heat the remaining oil in a roasting tin on the hob and brown the meat on all sides. Roast for 10 minutes, then remove from the tin and leave to rest in a warm place for 10 minutes. Discard the fat from the tin, add the red wine vinegar and stir well to deglaze the tin, then boil until the liquid has almost evaporated. Add the reserved stock and bring to the boil, then stir in half the redcurrant jelly and season to taste. You will have a slightly sweet yet peppery sauce. Stir in the blueberries and warm through.

Reheat the chestnut and celeriac purée then spoon it on to each serving plate. Cut the venison in slices about 6mm (¼ inch) thick and arrange on top. Spoon a little redcurrant jelly on to each pear quarter, garnish with a sprig of mint and place on the plates. Spoon some sauce over the meat and serve.

LEMON CRÊPE GÂTEAU

7 eggs

300g (10oz) caster sugar

180ml (6fl oz) lemon juice

60g (2oz) unsalted butter, diced

30g (1oz) powdered or leaf gelatine

100ml (3½fl oz) water

400ml (14fl oz) double cream, lightly whipped

icing sugar for dusting

For the crêpes

100g (3½oz) plain flour

pinch of salt

2 eggs

4 tbsp caster sugar

300ml (½ pint) milk

45g (1½oz) butter

The idea of cold pancakes may alarm you but they make a surprisingly good base for this unusual gâteau.

For the crêpes, sift the flour and salt into a large bowl, then add the eggs, sugar and about a quarter of the milk and mix to a thick batter. Slowly add the rest of the milk to give a thin pouring batter. If there are any lumps in it, pass it through a fine sieve. Melt the butter in a pan until it begins to foam and then whisk half of it into the batter. Leave to rest in a cool place for 15 minutes.

Heat a 20cm (8 inch) non-stick omelette pan, brush with a little of the remaining melted butter, then ladle in enough batter to cover the base of the pan in a thin layer, tilting the pan gently so the batter spreads evenly. Cook for 30 seconds over a medium-high heat until browned, then turn over and cook for a further 30 seconds. Continue making pancakes in this way until all the batter is used up. There should be 10 pancakes.

Place the eggs, sugar and lemon juice in a heavy-based pan and bring just to the boil over a gentle heat, whisking constantly. Remove from the heat and stir in the butter until it has melted.

Put the gelatine and water in a pan, soak for 10 minutes, then heat gently to dissolve. Add a little of the lemon mousse, mix well, then fold into the remaining mousse. Leave to cool. Fold in the lightly whipped cream.

Lightly grease the base and sides of a 23cm (9 inch) round spring-release tin, and line with cling film. Use 4–5 pancakes to line the base and sides of the tin, reserving 2 for the top, then layer the lemon mousse and remaining pancakes. Finish with one reserved pancake, fold in overlapping edges, and top with the other pancake. Cover and chill for at least 4 hours, preferably overnight, until set. Unmould and dust with icing sugar.

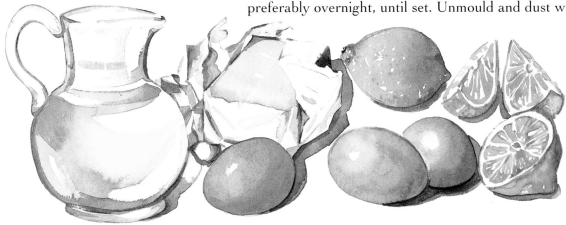

WINTER MENU ONE

AUBERGINE GRATIN
DUCK WITH MINTED TAGLIATELLE
MERINGUE-GLAZED APPLES IN CARAMEL SAUCE

AUBERGINE GRATIN

2 narrow aubergines

180g (6oz) raw chicken breast, diced

2 tbsp olive oil

2 tomatoes, blanched, peeled, deseeded
and diced

30g (1oz) Parmesan cheese, freshly grated

basil to garnish

For the tomato sauce

45g (1½oz) onion, finely chopped

3 tbsp groundnut oil

1 clove of garlic, peeled and chopped

200g (7oz) plum tomatoes, cut into quarters

20g (¾oz) tomato purée

200ml (7fl oz) chicken or vegetable stock

6 basil leaves, with stalks (optional)

salt and peppermill

Light and tasty, this is the perfect starter. You can use fillets of veal instead of chicken.

For the tomato sauce, sweat the onion in the oil until translucent. Add the garlic and sweat for a further minute. Add the tomatoes, tomato purée, stock and basil stalks and simmer, covered, for another 10 minutes. Pass through a fine sieve. Cut the basil leaves into strips and stir into the sauce. Season to taste.

Cut the aubergines in half lengthways and sprinkle with salt. Leave for 15 minutes, then rinse and dry. Heat the oven to 200°C/400°F/Gas Mark 6. Place the aubergines on a baking sheet and cook for 20–30 minutes, until tender. In the meantime, season the chicken and fry it very quickly in the oil, until sealed on all sides.

Remove the seeds from the aubergine and discard, then remove the aubergine flesh from the skin and chop. Mix the chicken and tomatoes with the aubergine·flesh and adjust the seasoning. Put the mixture in the aubergine skins, sprinkle with the Parmesan cheese and return to the oven for about 15 minutes. Alternatively, place under a hot grill until bubbling. Serve with tomato sauce and garnish with a little shredded basil and sprigs of basil.

DUCK WITH MINTED TAGLIATELLE

2 duck legs and 4 duck breasts

3 spring onions, cut into fine strips

1 small red chilli, seeds removed and finely diced

1 tsp freshly grated ginger

100ml (3½fl oz) soy sauce

2 tbsp Acacia honey

100ml (3½fl oz) yoghurt

8 x 20cm (8 inch) squares of filo pastry

1 egg yolk, beaten

1 tbsp groundnut oil

vegetable oil for deep frying

salt and peppermill

For the minted tagliatelle

150g (5oz) peas

200g (7oz) fresh tagliatelle

4 tbsp extra virgin olive oil

15g (½oz) bunch of mint, stalks removed, leaves chopped

3 tbsp freshly grated Parmesan cheese

TIP

At the Savoy we use peppered tagliatelle. If you are making your own pasta, crush about a tablespoon of black peppercorns very finely with a pestle and mortar and work them into the pasta dough.

Although there are quite a few strong flavours in this dish, it works beautifully.

You can prepare the duck legs a day in advance. Remove the skin from the duck legs, place them in a saucepan and cover with cold water, adding a generous pinch of salt. Simmer for 40 minutes until the duck is well done, skimming the surface of the water frequently. Remove the pan from the heat and leave to cool. Take out the duck legs, remove the meat from the bone and cut it into small cubes. Mix with the spring onions, chilli and half the ginger and season with salt and pepper.

Place the duck breasts on a work surface skin-side down. Clean and trim the protruding skin, then remove the sinews around the breast, turn over and score the skin in diagonal lines 1.5cm (½ inch) apart.

Mix together the soy sauce, honey, yoghurt and remaining ginger and marinate the duck breasts in this mixture for at least 10 minutes – they may be left for up to 24 hours in the fridge.

Heat the oven to 180°C/350°F/Gas Mark 4. Place 4 squares of filo on the work surface and brush with beaten egg yolk. Set another square of filo on top of each one and spoon the duck mixture into the centre. Brush the edges of the pastry with more egg yolk, bring the sides up over the filling and pinch together to make 'moneybag' shapes.

Heat the groundnut oil in a non-stick frying pan. Remove the breasts from the marinade and wipe them clean. Fry, skin-side down, over a high heat until the skin is evenly crispy then turn over and cook for a further few seconds. Transfer to a roasting tin and roast in the oven for about 10 minutes, or longer if you want the duck to be more than medium cooked. Remove from the pan and leave to rest for 8–10 minutes.

Heat the oil for deep frying to 170°C/325°F and fry the filo parcels in it for 2–3 minutes, until lightly browned. They will get darker after they have been removed from the oil. Drain on kitchen paper and keep warm.

Cook the peas in boiling, salted water until tender. Drain. Boil the tagliatelle in plenty of salted water for about 3 minutes until the pasta is *al dente*, then drain. Heat the olive oil in a large pan, add the pasta and peas and heat through. Add the mint and season with salt, pepper and the Parmesan cheese.

Place a filo parcel on each serving plate and spoon the pasta beside it. Cut the duck breasts into thick slices and place on top of the pasta.

AUBERGINE GRATIN, DUCK WITH MINTED TAGLIATELLE, AND MERINGUE-GLAZED APPLES IN CARAMEL SAUCE

MERINGUE-GLAZED APPLES IN CARAMEL SAUCE

2 Golden Delicious apples, peeled, halved
and cored

100ml (3½fl oz) dry white wine

1 clove

½ cinnamon stick

90g (3oz) caster sugar

1 tbsp liquid glucose

150ml (¼ pint) double cream

50g (1¾oz) unsalted butter

1 tbsp calvados (or brandy or whisky)

4 scoops of ice cream (flavour of your choice
but vanilla or nut goes well)

For the meringue

3 egg whites

140g (4½oz) caster sugar

Place the apple halves in a small, deep saucepan and add the white wine, spices, half the sugar and just enough water to cover. Bring slowly to the boil, then remove the apples and dry on a kitchen cloth. Reserve 100ml (3½fl oz) of the cooking liquid and place in a small, heavy-based pan with the remaining sugar and the glucose. Boil until reduced to a dark amber colour – be careful not to let it burn. Remove from the heat, stir in the cream and butter and add the calvados. Keep warm.

For the meringue, whisk the egg whites to stiff peaks, then whisk in the sugar a little at a time to make a firm, glossy meringue. Place the apples on a baking tray with the cavities facing up and top each one with a scoop of ice-cream, making sure it is frozen firm. Using a large star nozzle, pipe the meringue in a decorative pattern over the top of the apples and all over the ice cream to encase it completely. Place under a very hot grill until golden brown, about 1–2 minutes. (Blow torches are often used professionally to give a good, even, golden colouring.)

Pour a little of the warm sauce on to each serving plate and place an apple in the centre.

TIP

If you heat the sugar in the oven before adding it to the egg white for the meringue, it will dissolve more easily and there will be no solid sugar crystals in it.

NEW YEAR'S DAY MENU

SCALLOP AND POTATO SALAD
ROAST PHEASANT WITH A SOUR SHALLOT SAUCE
STICKY TOFFEE PUDDING

SCALLOP AND POTATO SALAD

4 courgettes, topped and tailed

2 carrots, peeled, topped and tailed

12 large scallops, shell and roe removed

12 rashers of thinly cut smoked streaky bacon

4 tbsp olive oil

6 medium new potatoes, cut into 6mm
(¼ inch) slices

4 cloves of garlic, peeled

2 sprigs of rosemary

45g (1½oz) butter

For the dressing

45g (1½oz) baby spinach or rocket

100ml (3½fl oz) olive oil

1½ tbsp balsamic vinegar

½ tsp lemon juice

salt and peppermill

TIP
Marinate the garlic in the oil for a few
days before starting the recipe.

**There are two types of scallops. The small ones are called Queen Scallops and these are good for garnishing dishes; the larger variety, Deep Sea Scallops, are good for grilling, frying or poaching.
Scallops, like most fish, taste better if slightly undercooked.**

For the dressing, place all the ingredients in a food processor and blend until smooth.

Using a vegetable peeler, peel ribbons from all 4 'sides' of each courgette, stopping when you reach the seeds. Repeat with the carrots, stopping before you reach the central core. Blanch all the vegetable ribbons in plenty of boiling salted water, then drain them and refresh in iced water.

Wrap each scallop in a rasher of bacon and secure with a cocktail stick. Heat 2 tablespoons of the oil in a non-stick pan, add the potatoes, the garlic and the sprigs of rosemary and fry until golden brown. Season half way through with salt and pepper. Add half the butter just before the end of the cooking. Remove from the heat and keep warm.

Fry the scallops in the remaining oil and butter until the bacon is crispy and the scallops are just done but still slightly undercooked.

Warm the vegetable ribbons in half the dressing in a pan, then season and place in the centre of each serving plate. Arrange the potatoes around the edge and the scallops on top. Pour a little more dressing over the potatoes and scallops just before serving.

ROAST PHEASANT WITH A SOUR SHALLOT SAUCE

2 oven-ready pheasants, breasts covered with streaky bacon

100ml (3½fl oz) groundnut oil

350g (12oz) floury potatoes, peeled and cut into large cubes

1 Savoy cabbage, outside leaves removed, finely shredded

45g (1½oz) onion, peeled and finely chopped

20g (¾oz) unsalted butter

2 small cloves of garlic, peeled and crushed

90g (3oz) smoked streaky bacon, finely diced

4 tbsp chicken stock or water

1 egg yolk

250g (8½oz) shallots, peeled and finely chopped

150ml (¼ pint) dry white wine

2 tbsp red wine vinegar

3 sprigs of tarragon, leaves removed and chopped

1 tbsp finely chopped parsley

1 plum tomato, blanched, peeled, deseeded and diced

salt, peppermill and nutmeg

TIPS

Always choose the hen pheasant. It is a little smaller than the male pheasant, yet the more tender of the two.

Pheasants of course, like other game birds, need hanging. But it is perhaps not something you would do at home, where probably the conditions are not quite right, so ask your game dealer to do it for you.

Pheasant is known to be low in cholesterol and healthy, yet the popularity of game on the whole, perhaps with the exception of venison, seems to be on the decline. To my mind, it has the most intensive flavour of any meat and by intensive, I do not mean that it is very gamey. I also think that ideally all game birds should be served off the bone, or at least jointed, so you can enjoy them without a fight!

Preheat the oven to 200°C/400°F/Gas Mark 6. Season the pheasants inside and out with salt and pepper. Heat 3 tablespoons of the oil in a roasting tin on the hob and brown the pheasants well on all sides. Transfer to the oven and roast for about 25 minutes by laying them for 10 minutes on one leg, then 10 minutes on the other. Remove the bacon and roast the birds breast-side up for the last 5 minutes. Remove the birds from the pan, keep them warm and rest them for 10 minutes.

Meanwhile, cook the potatoes from cold in salted water until tender. Drain and dry over a gentle heat or in the heat of the oven for 5 minutes, then pass through a fine sieve. Boil the cabbage in plenty of salted water for 2 minutes, then drain, refresh in cold water and squeeze dry.

Sweat the onion in the butter until translucent, add half the garlic and the bacon and cook until crispy. Add the cabbage and chicken stock or water and cook, uncovered, until all the liquid has evaporated and the cabbage is dry. Mix the potatoes with the cabbage, then stir in the egg yolk and season with salt, pepper and a little nutmeg. Form the mixture into 8 small cakes.

Sweat the shallots in 2 tablespoons of oil until translucent, add the remaining garlic and sweat for a further minute. Add the wine and vinegar and boil until reduced by three-quarters. Cool slightly, then pass through a mouli or work in a food processor until fairly smooth. Thin with a little chicken stock if necessary. Add the herbs and diced tomato and adjust the seasoning. Heat the remaining oil in a non-stick pan and fry the cakes until golden brown on both sides.

Place 2 potato cakes on each serving plate, take off the breasts and legs from the pheasants and place on top of the potato cakes. Serve with the sauce.

STICKY TOFFEE PUDDING

120g (4oz) unsalted butter

120g (4oz) soft brown sugar

4 eggs, separated

150g (5oz) plain flour

1 tsp baking powder

Sauce Anglaise (see below)

For the caramel sauce

50g (1¾oz) caster sugar

4 tbsp double cream

TIP

A small roasting tin is ideal to use as a bain-marie. Put the puddings in it and pour in hot water to come at least half way up the sides of the dariole moulds.

Preheat the oven to 180°C/350°F/Gas Mark 4. Grease 4 dariole moulds, 300ml (½ pint) each in capacity. Make the caramel sauce by melting the sugar in a saucepan over a high heat and then carefully stirring in the warmed cream. Pour a little of the caramel mixture into the bottom of each mould.

Cream the butter and sugar until pale and fluffy, then beat in the egg yolks. Sift the flour with the baking powder and beat into the mixture. Whisk the egg whites to soft peaks and fold them into the mixture. Divide between the moulds and cover with greased greaseproof paper that has been pleated in the centre, then kitchen foil. Bake in a bain-marie for about 40 minutes or until a knife inserted into the centre comes out clean. Turn out the puddings and serve with warm Sauce Anglaise.

SAUCE ANGLAISE

500ml (16fl oz) milk

1 vanilla pod, split

6 egg yolks

75g (2½oz) caster sugar

Put the milk and vanilla pod in a pan, bring almost to boiling point, then remove from the heat and leave to infuse for about 10 minutes. Whisk the egg yolks and sugar together until thick and pale. Bring the milk to the boil, pour it over the egg yolk mixture and mix thoroughly. Wash out the pan and return the custard to it. Stir gently with a wooden spoon over a low heat until the sauce thickens and coats the back of the spoon; do not let it boil. Leave to cool, then pass through a fine sieve.

WINTER MENU TWO

CREAM OF JERUSALEM ARTICHOKE SOUP WITH WATERCRESS
GRILLED SKIRT STEAK WITH GARLIC AND CHILLI DIP
CHOCOLATE AND NOUGAT PAVÉ

CREAM OF JERUSALEM ARTICHOKE SOUP WITH WATERCRESS

1 bunch of watercress

60g (2oz) shallots, peeled and finely chopped

60g (2oz) unsalted butter

2 cloves of garlic, peeled and chopped

400g (14oz) Jerusalem artichokes, peeled and
cut into cubes

1 sprig of thyme

4 tbsp white wine

900ml (1½ pints) chicken stock

4 tbsp crème fraîche or double cream

salt and peppermill

Jerusalem artichokes originate from North America and have a beautiful nut-like taste. They can be cooked in the same way as potatoes. Their season runs from autumn to spring.

Pick over the watercress and separate the stalks and large leaves from the small leaves. Sweat the shallots in the butter until translucent, then add the garlic and sweat for a further minute. Add the Jerusalem artichokes, watercress stalks and large watercress leaves, thyme, white wine and chicken stock. Season with salt and pepper and simmer gently, covered, until the artichokes are soft, skimming the surface frequently. Leave to cool, then purée in a food processor. Reheat gently and stir in the small watercress leaves and the cream. Adjust the seasoning to taste.

GRILLED SKIRT STEAK WITH GARLIC AND CHILLI DIP

8 cloves of garlic, peeled and crushed

12 green chillies, deseeded and

finely chopped

30g (1oz) bunch of coriander, stalks removed,

leaves chopped

6 tbsp olive oil

juice of 1 lemon

4 x 300g (10 oz) pieces of skirt steak

salt and peppermill

Skirt is a cut full of flavour and taste, not often used in this country. It comes very much into its own in France, where it is highly prized. Skirt steak has to be hanged well before use so you'd better know your butcher! It is usually cut thick and then cooked briefly at a very high temperature.

Combine the garlic, chillies, coriander, olive oil, lemon juice, and salt and pepper in a pestle and mortar or food processor and work to a pulp. Spread half the mixture in a thin layer on the steaks and leave to marinate for 15 minutes (or up to 24 hours in a cool place).

Heat the grill and grill the steak for about 5 minutes on each side, depending on the thickness of the meat and how well you like your steak done. Slice thickly against the grain of the meat and serve with the remaining dip.

CHOCOLATE AND NOUGAT PAVÉ

CHOCOLATE AND NOUGAT PAVÉ

300g (10oz) good-quality plain chocolate

450ml (¾ pint) double cream

75g (2½oz) blossom honey

90g (3oz) good-quality nougat (preferably Montélimar), cut in small pieces

white chocolate shavings to decorate

a little cocoa powder to decorate

Sauce Anglaise (see page 85), flavoured with Benedictine liqueur to taste

Planning ahead: Prepare the pavé a day in advance.

Line a 450g (1lb) loaf tin or terrine with cling film. Break up the chocolate and melt it in a bowl set over a pan of hot water. Whip the cream with the honey until semi-whipped and fold it into the cooled but still liquid chocolate, then stir in the chopped nougat. Transfer to the tin and level the surface. Leave in the fridge overnight to set. Unmould the pavé on to a plate, cover the top with the white chocolate shavings and dust with cocoa powder. Serve with the Sauce Anglaise.

TIP

Nougat is available in good confectionery shops. At The Savoy we make our own nougat, and we use the left-over trimmings for the pavé.

AFTERNOON TEA

The idea of afternoon tea has a powerful and enduring appeal. For me, it brings to mind images of a perfect summer afternoon in the English countryside. Beneath the branches of a willow tree a table is set with plates of exquisite French pastries, warm scones, clotted cream and strawberry jam. By some miracle, the elegantly dressed ladies enjoying this feast remain slender and slim-waisted.

In this vision of perfection, sweet flavours are balanced by savoury. As well as pastries there are wafer-thin cucumber, smoked salmon and tomato sandwiches. To refresh the palate a choice of teas from India, China and Ceylon is served in fine bone china.

In the city, the atmosphere of afternoon tea becomes subtly different. A piano plays discreetly in the background, while on a small dance floor couples take a little gentle exercise in the form of foxtrots and waltzes.

At fine hotels such as the Savoy and Claridges it is still possible to enjoy elegant and beautifully presented afternoon teas like the ones that were so appreciated by the Victorians. What is sometimes forgotten, however, is that the Victorians were great innovators. It is in a spirit of innovation that I have brought together the recipes in this chapter, drawing on the best American and Continental traditions. I have also learned from the British institution of 'high tea', a far more substantial event, which can include warm savouries and provide the main meal of the evening.

Afternoon tea is more than just a meal. Indeed, many of our guests at the Savoy use it as an opportunity to do business. Better still, afternoon tea is a chance to set the world to rights, a pleasant and civilized way to spend time talking or gossiping with friends.

AFTERNOON TEA MENUS

Here are a selection of menus, each containing both
savoury and sweet dishes. Using these as examples, you
can build your own menus to suit the occasion.

MENU 1
Diana's Puff Pastry Tartlets with Cèpes 95
Herb Scones with Smoked Salmon and
Keta Caviar 98
Creamed Avocado with Plum Tomato and Red
Onion Sandwiches 101
Chocolate Nirvana 115
Sienna Cake with Honeycomb 115
Strawberry Tartlets 105

MENU 2
Deep-fried Vegetable and Cheese
Wontons 94
Smoked Salmon with Crème Fraîche and Dill
Sandwiches 102
Saffron Scones with Raisins 104
Lemon Tartlets 107
Dried Fruit Tart with Streusel 112

MENU 3
Mediterranean Anchovy, Olive and
Onion Tart 98
Roast Beef with Horseradish Mayonnnaise
Sandwiches 101
Tangy Lemon Mousse Squares 114
Sacher Torte 109
Pear Frangipane Tarts 106

MENU 4
Chipolatas Filled with Garlic Potato
Purée 92
Prawn and Spring Onion with Cocktail Sauce
Sandwiches 102
Chocolate Tarts with Blood Oranges 112
Carrot Cake with Almonds 110
Exotic Fruit Tartlets 106

MENU 5
Russian Potato and Cabbage Pastries 95
Cheese Sablés 99
Chicken, Lettuce and Mayonnaise
Sandwiches 101
Coffee Gâteau 111
Pineapple Tarte Tatin 107

SUN-DRIED TOMATO 'SNAILS'

Makes 24

225g (8oz) plain flour
50g (1¾oz) unsalted butter
45g (1½oz) soft cheese
1 egg yolk
100g (3½oz) pecorino cheese, grated
90g (3oz) Home-dried Tomatoes in Olive Oil
(see page 30)
100g (3½oz) anchovy fillets, chopped
90g (3oz) pitted black olives, chopped

Planning ahead: The dough can be prepared a day in advance. Alternatively you can make the snails, then freeze and thaw them and bake whenever required.

Sift the flour into a bowl and rub in the butter and soft cheese until the mixture resembles fine crumbs. Add the egg yolk and sufficient cold water to form a soft, smooth dough. Wrap in cling film and refrigerate for 20 minutes. Preheat the oven to 200°C/400°F/Gas Mark 6.

On a lightly floured surface, roll out the dough to a 35 x 30cm (14 x 12 inch) rectangle. Sprinkle it evenly with the cheese, then arrange the remaining ingredients on top. Roll up the dough like a swiss roll, starting at a long side, and cut it into slices 1.5cm (½ inch) thick. Arrange on a greased baking tray and bake for about 20 minutes, until golden brown. Serve warm.

CHIPOLATAS FILLED WITH GARLIC POTATO PURÉE

200g (7oz) old potatoes, peeled and diced
1 clove of garlic, peeled
4 tbsp olive oil
1 tbsp milk
1 tbsp double cream
½ egg yolk
20 chipolatas
2 tsp French mustard
salt

Planning ahead: Prepare the chipolatas 2 hours in advance and fill them with the potato purée, then reheat in a moderate oven.

Wash the potatoes well to remove the starch, then place in a saucepan with cold water just to cover, with the garlic, a third of the olive oil and a generous pinch of salt. Cook until the potatoes are just tender but not mushy, then drain well. Transfer the garlic to a board and crush with the side of a knife. Heat 1 tablespoon of the remaining oil in a small frying pan and fry the garlic for 1 minute without colouring. Return the garlic to the potatoes and mash well.

Heat the milk, cream and remaining oil in a small saucepan and gradually mix into the mashed potato. Add the egg yolk, mixing it well with a wooden spoon. Grill the chipolatas until browned on all sides. Cut down the length of each one and open it out – do not cut completely in half. Smear a little mustard into each sausage then pipe the potato purée along each one using a fine nozzle. Return to the grill until the potato purée is slightly coloured.

A SELECTION OF SAVOURIES (SEE PAGES 92-95)

SWISS MUSHROOM RAREBIT

8 medium open-cap mushrooms

2 shallots, peeled and finely chopped

120g (4oz) unsalted butter

250g (8½oz) button mushrooms, finely chopped

100ml (3½fl oz) dry white wine

2 tbsp plain flour

200ml (7fl oz) milk

50g (1¾oz) Emmenthal cheese, grated

2 egg yolks

1 tsp Dijon mustard

1 tbsp double cream

cayenne pepper

Worcestershire sauce

4 slices of white bread

salt and peppermill

Wipe the open-cap mushrooms, remove the stalks and chop them finely, reserving the mushroom caps. Sweat the shallots in 45g (1½oz) of the butter until soft and translucent. Add the button mushrooms and chopped mushroom stalks and sweat for a further minute. Season with salt and pepper, then add a teaspoon of the white wine and cook slowly until all the liquid has evaporated.

Melt the remaining butter in a small, heavy-based pan and add the flour. Stir over a medium heat for 2 minutes, then add the remaining wine and the milk and stir continously. The mixture may curdle at this stage because of the wine but don't worry – keep cooking it! Simmer for 2–3 minutes, stirring frequently, to give a smooth sauce. If there are any lumps, pass the sauce through a fine sieve. Remove from the heat and add three-quarters of the grated cheese, plus the egg yolks, mustard and cream. Add cayenne pepper and Worcestershire sauce to taste.

Place the mushroom caps on an oiled baking sheet and fill with the mushroom mixture. Spoon some sauce over each one, sprinkle with the remaining cheese and cook under a preheated grill until well browned and bubbling. Toast the bread and cut it to the same size as the mushrooms. Place a mushroom on each piece of toast and serve at once.

DEEP-FRIED VEGETABLE AND CHEESE WONTONS

Makes 12

100g (3½oz) soft goats' cheese, rind removed, cut into small dice

6 sage leaves, roughly chopped

45g (1½oz) vegetables, such as carrots, leeks, peas, beans, celeriac, kohlrabi or tomatoes, cut into tiny dice, lightly blanched (not the tomatoes) and refreshed

12 wonton wrappers

1 egg, beaten

oil for deep frying

Wontons are great! Wonton wrappers are available from Chinese food stores and are very useful to keep in the fridge or freezer. You can use them like ravioli or tortellini, which saves you making pasta dough.

Planning ahead: These can be prepared up to 4 hours in advance.

Mix the goats' cheese with the sage and vegetables, then divide the mixture between the wonton wrappers, placing it in the centre of each one. Brush the edges with beaten egg, pull up the corners to encase the filling and press them together to seal firmly. Heat the oil to 190°C/375°F. Deep fry the wonton for 1–2 minutes or until lightly browned, then drain on kitchen paper and serve immediately.

RUSSIAN POTATO AND CABBAGE PASTRIES

Makes 20

150g (5oz) old potatoes, peeled and diced

45g (1½oz) unsalted butter

45g (1½oz) onion, peeled and finely chopped

2 tbsp groundnut oil

150g (5oz) cabbage, finely shredded

½ tsp caraway seeds

3 tbsp soured cream or crème fraîche

2 tbsp chopped dill

180g (6oz) puff pastry

1 egg, beaten

salt and peppermill

Boil the potatoes in salted water until tender but not mushy. Drain thoroughly and dry over the heat, then pass through a fine sieve and stir in the butter while they are still hot. Sweat the onion in the oil until soft and translucent. Add the cabbage and caraway seeds, season lightly and cook, covered, over a moderate heat until tender but still slightly crisp. Stir in the potato, cream or crème fraîche and dill and adjust seasoning. Leave to cool.

On a lightly floured surface, roll out the pastry about 3mm (⅛ inch) thick. Cut out 20 star shapes about 9cm (3½ inch) in diameter and place a teaspoonful of the mixture in the centre of each one. Brush the pastry edges with beaten egg, bring the pointed ends up over the filling and press them firmly together. Brush with beaten egg and leave to rest in a cool place for 15 minutes while you heat the oven to 200°C/400°F/Gas Mark 6. Bake the pastries for about 20 minutes, until golden brown. Serve warm.

DIANA'S PUFF PASTRY TARTLETS WITH CÈPES

Makes 4

100g (3½oz) puff pastry

6 medium-sized firm cèpes

½ shallot, peeled and finely chopped

30g (1oz) unsalted butter

1 clove of garlic, peeled and crushed

1 tbsp white wine vinegar

4 tbsp white wine

100ml (3½fl oz) chicken stock

4 tbsp double cream

½ tsp chopped tarragon

salt and peppermill

TIP

Any variety of mushroom may be used if cèpes are unavailable.

Planning ahead: Prepare the tartlets and filling in advance, then reheat gently and put them together at the last minute.

On a lightly floured surface, roll out the puff pastry thinly and use to line four 7.5cm (3 inch) tartlet tins. Line the pastry cases with greaseproof paper or kitchen foil and weight them down with baking beans, then leave to rest in a cool place for 15 minutes while you heat the oven to 200°C/400°F/Gas Mark 6. Bake for about 15 minutes, then remove the paper and beans and bake for a further 5 minutes until golden brown.

Carefully clean the cèpes, scraping off the dirt with a knife, but do not wash them. Cut into slices.

Sweat the shallot in the butter until soft and translucent, then add the garlic and sweat for a further minute. Add the cèpes and sweat for a minute longer, then season with salt and pepper. Remove the cèpes from the pan with a slotted spoon, leaving the juices in the pan. Add the vinegar and wine and boil until completely evaporated. Add the stock and boil until reduced by two-thirds. Add the cream and cook until slightly thickened, then return the cèpes to the sauce. Stir in the tarragon and adjust the seasoning. Spoon the mixture into the warm pastry cases.

AUBERGINE, GOATS' CHEESE AND PESTO TOASTS, HERB SCONES WITH SMOKED SALMON AND KETA CAVIAR (PAGE 98), MEDITERRANEAN ANCHOVY, OLIVE AND ONION TART (PAGE 98), AND CHEESE SABLÉS (PAGE 99)

AUBERGINE, GOATS' CHEESE AND PESTO TOASTS

2 long, narrow aubergines, sliced into rounds
6mm (¼ inch) thick

3 red peppers

2 garlic cloves, peeled and crushed

60g (2oz) unsalted butter, softened

½ French stick, cut into slices 6mm
(¼ inch) thick

olive oil for frying

2 small goats' cheeses, rind removed and
crumbled

4 tbsp Pesto (see below)

1 tbsp finely shredded basil

1 tbsp balsamic vinegar

salt and peppermill

Sprinkle the aubergines with salt and leave in a cool place for 30 minutes, then rinse and pat dry. Grill the red peppers until charred and blistered all over. Place in a bag until cool enough to handle, then peel, deseed and cut into small dice.

Beat the garlic with the softened butter. Spread the French bread on one side with the garlic butter and grill on both sides until golden brown.

Heat a little olive oil in a heavy-based frying pan, season the aubergine slices with pepper and fry until golden brown on both sides, cooking them in batches as necessary. Drain on kitchen paper.

Place 1–2 slices of aubergine on each slice of toast, arrange some red pepper squares and goats' cheese on top, then place under the grill until the cheese is lightly melted. Add a drizzle of pesto and return to the grill for 1 minute. Just before serving, top with the basil and sprinkle with the balsamic vinegar.

PESTO

60g (2oz) Parmesan cheese, freshly grated

60g (2oz) basil leaves

30g (1oz) parsley

30g (1oz) pine kernels

15g (½oz) walnuts

15g (½oz) pistachio nuts, blanched
and skinned

2 cloves of garlic, peeled and chopped

250ml (8fl oz) olive oil

salt and peppermill

Put the cheese, herbs, nuts and garlic in a food processor. Add half the oil and process until the ingredients are finely chopped. With the motor running, gradually add the remaining oil through the feed tube. Season to taste with salt and pepper and process again briefly.

HERB SCONES WITH SMOKED SALMON AND KETA CAVIAR

Makes 8

250g (8½oz) strong plain flour

15g (½oz) baking powder

75g (2½oz) unsalted butter

4 tsp chopped mixed herbs, such as basil,
rosemary, marjoram and oregano

120ml (4fl oz) milk

1 egg, beaten

100ml (3½fl oz) crème fraîche

4–8 slices of smoked salmon, cut into pieces

2 tsp keta (salmon) caviar

small handful of tiny lettuce leaves and sprigs
of dill to garnish

The scones can be frozen and then reheated and topped with all kinds of savoury morsels.

Preheat the oven to 200°C/400°F/Gas Mark 6. Sift the flour and baking powder together, then rub in the butter until the mixture resembles breadcrumbs. Stir in the herbs. Add the milk and work to a soft dough. On a lightly floured surface, roll out to 2cm (¾ inch) thick and stamp out 6cm (2½ inch) rounds with a cutter. Transfer to a greased baking sheet, brush the tops with beaten egg and bake for about 15 minutes, until risen and golden brown.

Let the scones cool to lukewarm, then cut them in half, top with a little crème fraîche and arrange the smoked salmon on top. Garnish with a little lettuce on the side, spoon the keta caviar on top and finish with a sprig of dill.

MEDITERRANEAN ANCHOVY, OLIVE AND ONION TART

100ml (3½fl oz) olive oil

800g (1¾lb) onions, peeled and finely sliced

2 cloves of garlic, peeled and crushed

1 sprig of rosemary

2 sprigs of thyme

2 tbsp caster sugar

½ tbsp white wine vinegar

400g (14oz) puff pastry

1 egg, separated

30g (1oz) Parmesan cheese, finely grated

50g (1¾oz) anchovy fillets, cut in half
lengthways

45g (1½oz) pitted black olives, sliced

1–2 tbsp capers

30g (1oz) Home-dried Tomatoes in Olive Oil
(see page 30)

salt and peppermill

Planning ahead: Cook the onions in advance, and roll out and rest the pastry.

Heat the oil in a heavy-based pan, add the onions and sweat for 15–20 minutes, until very soft and translucent. Add the garlic and herbs and sweat for a further minute. Stir in the sugar and vinegar and cook, stirring frequently, until all the liquid has evaporated. Leave to cool. Discard the herb stalks.

On a lightly floured surface, roll out the pastry to 6mm (¼ inch) thick and trim the edges to make a 30cm (12 inch) square. Lightly beat the egg yolk and brush it in a border around the pastry, 1.5cm (½ inch) in from the edges. Fold 2cm (¾ inch) of pastry over the egg wash to make a crust. Prick the base and leave for 20 minutes in a cool place. Heat the oven to 200°C/400°F/Gas Mark 6. Lightly beat the egg white and brush the pastry base with it, then bake for about 15 minutes, until lightly golden.

Spread the onion mixture over the pastry, then sprinkle with the Parmesan cheese and garnish with the anchovies, olives, capers and dried tomatoes. Brush the pastry border with more egg yolk and return to the oven for 20–25 minutes. Serve warm, cut into squares.

CHEESE SABLÉS

Makes about 20

150g (5oz) plain flour

150g (5oz) Parmesan cheese, freshly grated

150g (5oz) butter

1 egg yolk

Mix the flour and cheese together in a bowl, then work in the butter with your fingertips until evenly mixed. Work in the egg yolk to form a firm dough. Wrap the dough and leave to rest in a cool place for about 30 minutes. Preheat the oven to 200°C/400°F/Gas Mark 6.

On a lightly floured surface, roll out the dough until it is about 6mm (¼ inch) thick. Stamp out 6cm (2½ inch) rounds and place on baking sheets. Bake for about 20 minutes, until golden, then cool on a wire rack.

MEDITERRANEAN VEGETABLE TURNOVERS

Makes 4

2 red peppers

3 tbsp olive oil

1 onion, peeled and finely chopped

2 cloves of garlic, peeled and crushed

100g (3½oz) button mushrooms, quartered

2 medium courgettes, cut in 1cm (⅓ inch) cubes

1 sprig of rosemary

½ tsp sugar

1 tsp white wine vinegar

4 plum tomatoes, blanched, peeled, deseeded and cut into large dice

400g (14oz) puff pastry

1 egg, beaten

salt and peppermill

TIP

For a better colour, use egg yolk mixed with a little water to glaze, and brush the pastries twice.

Planning ahead: The vegetable filling can be prepared a day in advance, and the turnovers can be assembled 2 hours before baking.

Put the peppers under a preheated grill until the skin is black and blistered. Place them in a bag until cool enough to handle, then peel, deseed and cut into 1cm (⅓inch) squares.

Heat the olive oil in a pan, add the onion and sweat until soft and translucent. Add the garlic and sweat for a further minute, then add the mushrooms and courgettes and cook for 2 minutes, stirring occasionally. Add the red peppers, rosemary, sugar and vinegar and season with salt and pepper. Cook over a medium heat for 10 minutes, stirring occasionally. Halfway through cooking, add the tomatoes to the pan and adjust the seasoning. Remove from the heat, discard the rosemary and leave to cool.

On a lightly floured surface, roll out the pastry to 3mm (⅛ inch) thick. Cut out four 10cm (4 inch) rounds and four 18cm (7 inch) rounds. Leave in a cool place for 15 minutes. Preheat the oven to 220°C/425°F/Gas Mark 7.

Use the large pastry rounds to line four 10cm (4 inch) diameter ramekin dishes, 175ml (6fl oz) in capacity, and fill with the vegetable mixture. Brush the edges of the pastry with beaten egg and place the smaller pastry rounds on top. Invert the pastries on to a baking sheet, remove the ramekins and, with the back of a knife, score half-circles about 6mm (¼ inch) apart, radiating out from the centre to the edge. Crimp the edges and make an air vent in the top of each one. Brush with beaten egg and bake for 20–25 minutes, until golden brown. Serve warm.

SPINACH AND FETA ECCLES

Makes 4

20g (¾oz) unsalted butter

30g (1oz) apple, peeled and finely chopped

1 tsp lemon juice

½ onion, peeled and finely chopped

2 tbsp vegetable oil

50g (1¾oz) spinach, blanched, squeezed dry and roughly chopped

90g (3oz) feta cheese, crumbled

45g (1½oz) raisins

200g (7oz) puff pastry

1 egg, beaten

salt and peppermill

When I first thought about savoury Eccles cakes, I didn't know what to expect. Spinach and feta was the first variety we tried and we now make them with many different fillings.

Melt the butter in a small pan, add the apple and lemon juice and sweat until softened. In a separate pan, sweat the onion in the oil until soft and translucent, then add the spinach and season with salt and pepper. Leave to cool, then stir in the feta, apple and raisins.

On a lightly floured surface, roll out the puff pastry to about 3mm (⅛ inch) thick and stamp out four 15cm (6 inch) rounds. Divide the filling between the pastry rounds, brush the edges with water, then fold the pastry over the filling to encase it completely and seal firmly. Turn the pastries over so that the seams are underneath, then roll until they are about 2.5cm (1 inch) deep. Brush the tops with beaten egg and make 2 small cuts in each one. Place the pastries on a greased baking tray and leave to rest in a cool place for 15 minutes while you heat the oven to 200°C/400°F/Gas Mark 6. Bake the pastries for about 20 minutes, until golden brown. Serve warm.

HONEY AND HAM BISCUITS

Makes about 16

20g (¾oz) onion, finely chopped

½ tsp olive oil

2 cloves of garlic, peeled and crushed

45g (1½oz) unsalted butter

1 tsp English mustard

1 egg yolk

4 tsp Acacia honey

50g (1¾oz) cooked ham, finely chopped

45g (1½oz) Cheddar cheese, grated

90g (3oz) plain flour

Sweat the onion in the oil until soft and translucent. Add the garlic and sweat for a further minute, then leave to cool. Beat the butter until creamy and then stir in the mustard and egg yolk. Add the onion and garlic, the honey, ham, cheese and flour, and mix until evenly combined. Wrap in cling film and chill for 20 minutes. Preheat the oven to 190°C/375°F/Gas Mark 5.

Roll out the dough on a lightly floured surface to 6mm (¼ inch) thick and stamp out 6cm (2½ inch) rounds. Place on a greased baking tray and bake for about 20 minutes, until golden. Cool on a wire rack.

SANDWICHES

ROAST BEEF WITH HORSERADISH MAYONNAISE

2 tbsp mayonnaise

2 tsp finely grated fresh horseradish

2 buttered slices of white bread

3 slices of roast beef

salt and peppermill

Mix the mayonnaise and horseradish together and spread evenly over both slices of bread. Fill with the roast beef and season to taste. Cut off the crusts and cut into 3 fingers.

CHICKEN, LETTUCE AND MAYONNAISE

2 tbsp mayonnaise

curry paste

½ cooked chicken breast, diced

2 buttered slices of white bread

¼ Little Gem lettuce, cut in fine strips

salt and peppermill

Mix the mayonnaise with curry paste to taste, then add the chicken and season with salt and pepper. Make a sandwich with the bread, filling it with the chicken mixture and lettuce. Cut off the crusts and cut into 3 fingers.

TOMATO AND RED ONION

1 plum tomato, blanched, peeled and sliced

½ small red onion, peeled and thinly sliced

2 buttered slices of white bread

¼ tsp white wine vinegar

salt and peppermill

Use the tomato and onion to fill the sandwich, sprinkling the onion with vinegar and seasoning with salt and pepper. Cut off the crusts and cut into 3 fingers.

CREAMED AVOCADO WITH PLUM TOMATO AND RED ONION

½ avocado, peeled and stoned

2 tbsp crème fraîche

½ plum tomato, blanched, peeled, deseeded and finely diced

¼ small red onion, peeled and finely chopped

2 buttered slices of brown bread

salt and peppermill

Mash the avocado with the crème fraîche. Stir in the diced tomato and red onion and season to taste. Fill the bread with this mixture to make a sandwich. Cut off the crusts and cut into 3 fingers.

COTTAGE CHEESE AND PINEAPPLE

75g (2½oz) cottage cheese
50g (1¾oz) pineapple, finely diced
2 buttered slices of brown bread
peppermill

Mix together the cottage cheese and pineapple and then season with freshly milled pepper. Make into a sandwich with the bread, cut off the crusts and cut into 3 fingers.

SMOKED SALMON WITH CRÈME FRAÎCHE AND DILL

2 tbsp crème fraîche
1 tbsp chopped dill
2 buttered slices of brown bread
2 thin slices of smoked salmon
peppermill

Mix together the crème fraîche and dill. Spread over both slices of bread then fill the sandwich with the smoked salmon and season with pepper. Cut off the crusts and cut into 3 fingers.

FETA CHEESE AND TOMATO

2 buttered slices of brown bread
1 plum tomato, blanched, peeled and sliced
2 thin slices of feta cheese
peppermill

Make a sandwich with the bread, filling it with the tomato slices and cheese. Season with pepper. Cut off the crusts and cut into 3 fingers.

BLACK OLIVE TAPENADE WITH CRÈME FRAÎCHE AND LETTUCE LEAVES

2 tbsp black olive tapenade
2 tsp crème fraîche
2 buttered slices of white bread
mixed lettuce leaves
peppermill

Mix the tapenade with the crème fraîche and spread over both slices of bread. Fill the sandwich with lettuce leaves and season with pepper. Cut off the crusts and cut into 3 fingers.

PRAWN AND SPRING ONION WITH COCKTAIL SAUCE

100g (3½oz) peeled prawns
2 spring onions, finely chopped
2 tbsp cocktail sauce
2 buttered slices of brown bread
salt and peppermill

Mix together the prawns, spring onions and cocktail sauce and season with salt and pepper. Make into a sandwich with the bread. Cut off the crusts and cut into 3 fingers.

Sandwich Selection, Saffron Scones with Raisins (page 104), Strawberry Tartlets (page 105),
Pear Frangipane Tarts and Exotic Fruit Tartlets (page 106)

SOFT ROE BARQUETTES

50g (1¾oz) plain flour

pinch of salt

30g (1oz) unsalted butter

4 x 15g (½oz) pieces of herring roe

2 thin rashers of smoked bacon, cut in

half crossways

1 tbsp peas, blanched

4 small sage leaves

3 tbsp double cream

½ egg, beaten

salt and peppermill

Sift the flour and salt together and rub in the butter until it resembles fine breadcrumbs, then mix to a firm dough with 1–2 teaspoons of iced water. Wrap in cling film and leave to rest in the fridge for 10 minutes. Roll out the pastry and use to line 4 barquette moulds. Rest them for 10 minutes. Preheat the oven to 200°C/400°F/Gas Mark 6. Line the pastry moulds with greaseproof paper and fill with baking beans, then bake for 10 minutes. Remove the paper and baking beans and bake for a further 5 minutes. Remove from the oven and reduce the temperature to 150°C/300°F/Gas Mark 2.

Wrap each piece of roe in bacon and grill until the bacon is crisp. Place one in the centre of each barquette. Sprinkle the peas into the barquettes and top with a sage leaf. Beat the cream with the egg and season with salt and pepper. Pour this mixture into the barquettes and bake for 10–15 minutes, until just set.

SAFFRON SCONES WITH RAISINS

Makes 8

generous pinch of saffron threads

150ml (¼ pint) white wine

250g (8½oz) strong plain flour

15g (½oz) baking powder

45g (1½oz) caster sugar

75g (2½oz) unsalted butter

100–120ml (3½–4fl oz) milk

60g (2oz) raisins

1 egg, beaten

butter or clotted cream to serve

Saffron brings richness and flavour to scones. Topped with clotted cream and soft fruit they are a real luxury.

Planning ahead: The scones can be frozen and then reheated before serving.

Preheat the oven to 200°C/400°F/Gas Mark 6. Put the saffron and wine in a small saucepan and boil until reduced to 1 tablespoonful. Pass through a fine sieve.

Sift the flour and baking powder together, then stir in the sugar. Rub in the butter until the mixture resembles breadcrumbs. Add the saffron liquid and sufficient milk to form a soft, smooth dough, then work in the raisins. On a lightly floured surface, roll out the dough to 2cm (¾ inch) thick and stamp out 6cm (2½ inch) rounds with a cutter. Transfer to a greased baking sheet, brush the tops with beaten egg and bake for about 15 minutes until risen and golden brown.

Cut in half and serve with butter or clotted cream. Alternatively, spread with a little clotted cream and top with fresh fruit in season and a tiny sprig of mint.

STRAWBERRY TARTLETS

Makes 4

3 sheets of filo pastry

20g (¾oz) unsalted butter, melted

½ quantity of Frangipane (see page 70)

2 tsp crème de framboise liqueur (optional)

4 tbsp pastry cream (see below) or
whipped cream

14 medium strawberries, hulled

4 tbsp strawberry jam, warmed and sieved,
for glazing

a few skinned and chopped pistachio nuts
to decorate

Brush one sheet of filo pastry with melted butter. Lay another sheet on top and brush with more butter, then add the final sheet and brush again. Cut out four 9–10cm (3½–4 inch) rounds and use to line four 7.5cm (3 inch) tartlet tins. Heat the oven to 200°C/400°F/Gas Mark 6. Divide the frangipane between the pastry cases and bake for about 10 minutes, until golden. Leave to cool.

Stir the framboise liqueur, if using, into the pastry cream or whipped cream and spoon it into the centre of each tartlet, keeping it away from the edges or it will flow out when the fruit is pressed on. Place a whole strawberry in the centre of each tart, cut the rest in half and arrange around the whole ones. Brush with strawberry jam to glaze and then sprinkle a few chopped pistachios on top.

PASTRY CREAM

150ml (¼ pint) milk

¼ vanilla pod, split and seeds scraped out

1 egg yolk

20g (¾oz) caster sugar

20g (¾oz) plain flour, sifted

Planning ahead: This will keep in the fridge for 2–3 days. If you make it in advance, be sure to chill it quickly and thoroughly.

Put the milk, vanilla pod and seeds in a pan and bring to the boil over a gentle heat. Whisk the egg yolk and sugar together until pale and creamy. Add the flour and mix to a smooth paste. Pour on half the boiling milk and mix well. Return the mixture to the pan with the remaining milk, stirring constantly, and boil for 1 minute until thickened. Pass through a fine sieve.

WALNUT PIE

250g (8½oz) Sweet Pastry (see page 37)

300g (10oz) walnuts, shelled

3 eggs

150g (5oz) soft brown sugar

75g (2½oz) unsalted butter, melted

100g (3½oz) golden syrup

Preheat the oven to 170°C/325°F/Gas Mark 3. On a lightly floured surface, roll out the pastry and use to line a deep 20cm (8 inch) flan tin. Reserve 50g (1¾oz) of the walnut halves, then coarsely blend the rest in a food processor with the eggs, sugar, melted butter and syrup. Pour into the pastry case and arrange the reserved walnut halves on top. Bake for about 1 hour, until the filling is set.

PEAR FRANGIPANE TARTS

Makes 4

250g (8½oz) caster sugar
500ml (16fl oz) water
a few drops of lemon juice
1 cinnamon stick
½ vanilla pod
1 large pear, peeled, quartered and cored
120g (4oz) Sweet Pastry (see page 37)
4 tsp raspberry jam
Frangipane (see page 70)
4 tbsp apricot jam, warmed and sieved,
for glazing

Planning ahead: The pastry, frangipane and poached pears can all be prepared a day in advance.

Preheat the oven to 200°C/400°F/Gas Mark 6. Put the sugar and water in a saucepan and heat until the sugar has dissolved, then add the lemon juice, cinnamon stick and vanilla pod and bring to the boil. Add the pear quarters and simmer until just tender. Remove from the syrup and leave to cool, then slice through each pear quarter, leaving the slices joined together at the pointed end so they can be fanned out.

On a lightly floured surface, roll out the pastry to 3mm (⅛ inch) thick and use to line 4 deep 7.5cm (3 inch) tartlet tins. Place a teaspoon of raspberry jam in each one. Divide the frangipane between them, then top with a pear fan. Bake for about 20 minutes, until the frangipane is golden brown. Leave to cool, then glaze with the apricot jam.

EXOTIC FRUIT TARTLETS

Makes 4

100g (3½oz) puff pastry
½ quantity of Frangipane (see page 70)
1 tbsp passion fruit juice, sieved
4 tbsp Pastry Cream (see page 105) or
whipped cream
½ kiwi fruit, peeled and sliced
¼ mango, peeled, stoned and sliced
¼ small pineapple, peeled, cored and sliced
¼ pawpaw, peeled, deseeded and sliced
4 tbsp apricot jam, warmed and sieved,
for glazing
4 tiny sprigs of mint

You can fill these tarts with any fruit in season.

Planning ahead: The tartlets can be prepared in advance, then filled with the cream and fruit a few hours in advance.

On a lightly floured surface, roll out the puff pastry thinly and use to line four 7.5cm (3 inch) tartlet tins. Leave to rest in a cool place for 15 minutes. Preheat the oven to 200°C/400°F/Gas Mark 6. Divide the frangipane between the pastry cases and bake for 10–15 minutes until golden brown. Leave to cool.

Stir the passion fruit juice into the pastry cream or whipped cream and spoon it into the tartlets. Arrange the fruit on top, brush with apricot jam, then decorate with the mint.

PINEAPPLE TARTE TATIN

Makes 8

1 large pineapple
100g (3½oz) caster sugar
120g (4oz) unsalted butter
2 tbsp chopped preserved stem ginger
120g (4oz) plain flour
½ tsp bicarbonate of soda
½ tsp baking powder
pinch of salt
150g (5oz) soft brown sugar
2 eggs
1 tsp vanilla extract
100ml (3½fl oz) crème fraîche

The caramel works well with the tartness of the pineapple in this new twist on an old favourite.

Butter 8 deep 10cm (4 inch) ramekin dishes and, if you wish, line the bases with baking parchment. Preheat the oven to 190°C/375°F/Gas Mark 5. Peel the pineapple, cut it in half crossways, remove the core and cut it into 8 slices about 1.5cm (½ inch) thick. Trim them so they will fit exactly in the base of the ramekins. Reserve all the little bits of pineapple – you should have 150–200g (5–7oz) finely chopped bits.

Put the caster sugar in a heavy-based saucepan with a third of the butter and cook until it is a medium deep brown colour. Divide this caramel between the ramekin dishes and sprinkle with the chopped ginger. Set a slice of pineapple on top of each one.

Sift the flour, bicarbonate of soda, baking powder and salt together. Beat together the brown sugar and the remaining butter until creamy. Beat in the eggs one at a time, then add the vanilla extract. Fold in the flour mixture until well combined and then stir in the crème fraîche and reserved pineapple pieces. Divide the mixture between the ramekins, level the surface and bake for about 25 minutes, until firm. Leave until the dishes are cool enough to handle, then unmould carefully. Serve warm.

LEMON TARTLETS

Makes 16

150g (5oz) Sweet Pastry (see page 37)
100g (3½oz) caster sugar
3 eggs
finely grated zest of 2 lemons
2 tbsp lemon juice
75g (2½oz) unsalted butter, cut into cubes

Roll out the pastry on a lightly floured surface and use to line 16 tartlet tins, 5cm (2 inch) wide and 2cm (¾ inch) deep. Line with greaseproof paper and fill with baking beans, then chill for 20 minutes while you heat the oven to 200°C/400°F/Gas Mark 6. Bake the pastry cases for 10 minutes, then remove the paper and beans and bake for a further 5 minutes, until golden brown.

For the lemon filling, place the sugar, eggs, lemon zest and juice in a saucepan and cook over a gentle heat, whisking constantly, until the mixture thickens – do not let it boil or it will curdle. Remove from the heat and whisk in the butter a few pieces at a time. Leave to cool, then pipe or spoon the filling into the tartlet cases.

SACHER TORTE, PINEAPPLE TARTE TATIN (PAGE 107), AND BAKED CHOCOLATE CHEESECAKE (PAGE 110)

SACHER TORTE

140g (4½oz) unsalted butter, softened

100g (3½oz) icing sugar, sifted

1 vanilla pod, split and seeds scraped out

6 eggs, separated

120g (4oz) good-quality plain chocolate, melted

120g (4oz) plain flour, sifted

100g (3½oz) caster sugar

300g (10oz) orange marmalade, warmed and sieved

a little melted chocolate to decorate (optional)

For the chocolate glaze

5 tbsp milk

4 tbsp double cream

5 tbsp sugar syrup (see below)

4 tsp liquid glucose

300g (10oz) good-quality plain chocolate, chopped

Sacher Torte is always eaten with a cup of coffee — in this country that could easily be tea.

Planning ahead: You can make the cake a day in advance and then glaze it 2–3 hours before serving.

Preheat the oven to 170°C/325°F/Gas Mark 3. Grease and line a 23cm (9 inch) round cake tin. Beat the butter and icing sugar together with the vanilla seeds until pale, then beat in the egg yolks one at a time. Fold in the cooled melted chocolate and then the flour until evenly combined. In a separate bowl, whisk the egg whites until they form soft peaks, then whisk in the caster sugar a spoonful at a time until the mixture is stiff and glossy. Add a large spoonful to the chocolate mixture and fold in completely, then pour the chocolate mixture into the egg whites and fold in gently but thoroughly. Transfer the mixture to the prepared tin, level the surface and bake for about 45 minutes, until risen and just firm to the touch. Test by inserting a fine skewer into the centre of the cake; it will come out clean when the cake is cooked. Leave in the tin until cool enough to handle, then turn out on to a wire rack and leave to cool completely.

Cut the cake in half horizontally, then sandwich it together with about half the marmalade. Use the rest to cover the top and sides of the cake.

For the glaze, place the milk, cream, sugar syrup and glucose in a saucepan and bring to the boil. Remove from the heat and add the chocolate. Stir until melted and smooth. Allow to cool slightly.

Place the cake on a wire rack set over a tray and spread the chocolate glaze quickly all over the top and sides with a palette knife. Leave in a cool place to set. If wished, pipe 'Sacher' in melted chocolate on top of the cake.

SUGAR SYRUP

Makes about 600ml (1 pint)

250g (8½oz) caster sugar

500ml (16fl oz) water

a few drops of lemon juice

Put the sugar and water in a saucepan and dissolve over a gentle heat, swirling the pan occasionally. Add the lemon juice and bring to the boil. Boil for 1 minute and then leave to cool. The syrup will keep in the fridge for 1–2 weeks.

BAKED CHOCOLATE CHEESECAKE

250g (8½oz) Sweet Pastry (see page 37)

200g (7oz) quark or cream cheese

3 tbsp cocoa powder

60g (2oz) caster sugar

1 egg

150ml (¼ pint) double cream

75g (2½oz) good-quality plain chocolate, melted

finely grated zest of ½ orange

TIP

This looks good with a border of orange or ruby grapefruit segments and sprinkled with caramelized zest (see page 117).

Quark is now available in most supermarkets, but you could use cream cheese or, in a tight spot, sieved cottage cheese as a substitute.

Planning ahead: You can prepare the zest and segments the day before and the cake 4 hours in advance.

On a lightly floured surface, roll out the pastry and use to line a deep 20cm (8 inch) flan tin. Line with greaseproof paper, fill with baking beans and chill for 20 minutes while you heat the oven to 200°C/400°F/Gas Mark 6. Bake the pastry case for 10 minutes, then remove the paper and baking beans and bake for 10 minutes longer. Leave to cool. Reduce the oven temperature to 180°C/350°F/Gas Mark 4.

Beat the cheese, cocoa powder, sugar and egg until smooth, then stir in the cream. Fold the cooled melted chocolate and the orange zest into the mixture and transfer to the pastry case. Bake for about 20 minutes, until just set, then leave to cool.

CARROT CAKE WITH ALMONDS

120g (4oz) stale white breadcrumbs

4 egg yolks

120g (4oz) caster sugar

¼ tsp vanilla extract

1 tbsp lemon juice

finely grated zest of ½ lemon

150g (5oz) carrots, peeled and finely grated

90g (3oz) ground almonds

30g (1oz) blanched almonds, roughly chopped

½ tsp baking powder

¼ tsp ground allspice

pinch of salt

3 egg whites

¼ tsp cream of tartar

icing sugar for dusting

Planning ahead: This can be baked a day in advance and stored in an airtight container.

Preheat the oven to 200°C/400°F/Gas Mark 6. Butter a 20cm (8 inch) round cake tin and coat with some of the breadcrumbs. Mix the egg yolks, sugar, vanilla extract and lemon juice and zest in a food processor or with a hand-held electric mixer until the mixture looks slightly pale and is thick enough to coat the back of a spoon. Mix the grated carrots and all the almonds with the remaining breadcrumbs, the baking powder, allspice and salt and fold them into the egg yolk mixture with a spoon.

Whisk the egg whites with the cream of tartar until they form soft peaks and then fold them gently but thoroughly into the carrot mixture. Transfer to the prepared cake tin and bake for 30–40 minutes, until risen and firm to the touch. Turn out on to a wire rack to cool. Dust with icing sugar before serving.

COFFEE GÂTEAU

1 sponge cake (see page 114)

90g (3oz) milk chocolate, melted

3 gelatine leaves

250ml (8fl oz) milk

30g (1oz) freshly ground coffee

3 egg yolks

350ml (12fl oz) double cream

100g (3½oz) caster sugar

3 tbsp dark rum

100ml (3½fl oz) fresh strong black coffee

100ml (3½fl oz) sugar syrup (see page 109)

cocoa powder for dusting

Planning ahead: This can be prepared a day in advance, then turned out shortly before serving.

Cut the sponge to a 18cm (7 inch) round (keep the trimmings for a trifle), then cut it horizontally into 3 equal layers. Cut a strip of silicone paper to fit exactly round the inside of a deep 20cm (8 inch) round cake tin. Spread the melted chocolate evenly over the paper with a palette knife, then leave to firm slightly but not set. It should still be malleable. Carefully line the inside of the tin with the chocolate paper so the paper is against the sides of the tin. Chill until set.

For the coffee mousse, soak the gelatine leaves in cold water to cover for 10 minutes. Put the milk and ground coffee in a pan and bring to the boil, then remove from the heat and leave to infuse for 5 minutes. Pour through a piece of muslin and then pour on to the egg yolks, stirring constantly. Squeeze the excess water out of the gelatine and then add the warm milk mixture, stirring until the gelatine is completely dissolved.

Heat 4 tablespoons of the cream. Heat the sugar in a heavy-based pan until it dissolves and turns into a rich golden caramel. Take it off the heat, stir in the hot cream and then the milk mixture. Stir in half the rum. Pass the mixture through a fine sieve and leave to cool until just setting. Lightly whip the remaining cream and fold into the coffee mixture. Set aside.

Mix together the black coffee, sugar syrup and remaining rum. Drizzle this coffee syrup over each layer of sponge until they are thoroughly moistened. Place a layer of sponge in the cake tin. Pour in a third of the coffee mousse, top with a layer of sponge and then continue with the rest of the sponge and mousse. Chill in the fridge for at least 4 hours, preferably overnight, until set firm.

Carefully unmould the gâteau and peel away the paper, then dust the top liberally with cocoa powder.

CHOCOLATE TARTS WITH BLOOD ORANGES

Makes 4

120g (4oz) Sweet Pastry (see page 37)

90g (3oz) good-quality plain chocolate

60g (2oz) unsalted butter

1 egg

1 egg yolk

15g (½oz) caster sugar

16 blood orange segments, or caramelized

orange segments (see page 117)

4 sprigs of mint

Roll out the pastry and use to line four deep 7.5cm (3 inch) tartlet tins. Prick the bases, line with greaseproof paper or foil and fill with baking beans, then chill for at least 20 minutes while you heat the oven to 200°C/400°F/Gas Mark 6. Bake for 10 minutes, then remove the paper and beans and return to the oven for a further 5 minutes, until golden brown. Remove from the oven and leave to cool. Reduce the temperature to 150°C/1300°F/Gas Mark 2.

Melt the chocolate and butter in a bowl set over a pan of hot water until smooth and just warm to the touch. Whisk the egg, egg yolk and sugar together until thick, light and frothy, then fold in the chocolate mixture. Spoon into the pastry cases and bake for about 10 minutes, until lightly set. Remove from the oven and leave to cool completely. Just before serving, decorate with the blood orange segments and mint sprigs.

DRIED FRUIT TART WITH STREUSEL

250g (8½oz) Sweet Pastry (see page 37)

75g (2½oz) dried apricots, diced

75g (2½oz) prunes, diced

75g (2½oz) dried figs, diced

75g (2½oz) sultanas

3 tbsp Amaretto liqueur

For the custard layer

½ vanilla pod

2 egg yolks

45g (1½oz) caster sugar

100ml (3½fl oz) double cream

For the streusel

60g (2oz) plain flour

50g (1¾oz) caster sugar

50g (1¾oz) unsalted butter

30g (1oz) ground almonds

1 tsp ground allspice

On a lightly floured surface, roll out the pastry to about 3mm (⅛ inch) thick and use to line a deep 20cm (8 inch) flan tin. Line the pastry case with greaseproof paper or kitchen foil and weight it down with baking beans, then leave to rest in a cool place for 15 minutes while you heat the oven to 190°C/375°F/Gas Mark 5. Bake for 15 minutes, then remove the paper and beans and bake for a further 5 minutes, until golden brown.

Meanwhile, put the dried fruit, Amaretto and 5 tablespoons of water in a pan and simmer for 5 minutes. Leave to cool, by which time all the liquid will have been absorbed into the fruit.

Remove the pastry case from the oven and reduce the temperature to 180°C/350°F/Gas Mark 4.

For the custard layer, scrape the seeds from the vanilla pod and mix with the remaining ingredients. Spread the dried fruit over the base of the pastry case and pour the custard on top. Bake for 15 minutes.

For the streusel, mix all the ingredients together in a food processor, or rub them in by hand, until they resemble breadcrumbs. Sprinkle the streusel over the tart and return it to the oven for 15 minutes, until the topping is crisp. Serve warm or cold.

CHOCOLATE TARTS WITH BLOOD ORANGES

TANGY LEMON MOUSSE SQUARES

Makes 16

6 gelatine leaves

250ml (8fl oz) fresh lemon juice

finely grated zest of 4 lemons

140g (4½oz) caster sugar

500ml (16fl oz) double cream, whipped

60g (2oz) good-quality plain
chocolate, melted

4 tbsp sugar syrup (see page 109)

1 tbsp gin

200ml (7fl oz) clear lemon jelly (optional)

a little melted chocolate to decorate (optional)

For the sponge

4 eggs

100g (3½oz) caster sugar

100g (3½oz) plain flour, sifted

20g (¾oz) unsalted butter, melted

TIP

These could also be served as a dessert
for lunch or dinner.

Planning ahead: The sponge cake can be prepared up to 2 days in advance, then wrapped and stored in an airtight container. The squares can be prepared a day before serving, then turned out and cut up 6 hours in advance.

First make the sponge. Grease and flour a 20cm (8 inch) square cake tin and line the base with greaseproof paper. Preheat the oven to 190°C/375°F/Gas Mark 5. Put the eggs and sugar in a bowl set over a pan of simmering water and whisk until they have increased by 4 times their original volume. Gently fold in the sifted flour, then the cooled melted butter, and transfer to the tin. Bake for about 25 minutes, until risen and firm to the touch, then turn out on to a wire rack and leave to cool.

For the lemon mousse, soak the gelatine leaves in cold water to cover while you make a lemon syrup. Combine 200ml (7fl oz) of the lemon juice with the zest and sugar in a heavy-based saucepan. Bring slowly to the boil, stirring until the sugar has dissolved, then remove from the heat and leave to stand for 30 minutes.

Squeeze the water out of the gelatine and add it to the warm lemon syrup. Stir occasionally – it will dissolve in the heat – then pass through a fine sieve into a bowl. Put it over a pan of iced water, stirring occasionally to stop it setting around the sides. When cool, fold in the whipped cream.

Trim the edges of the cake, then cut it into 3 layers horizontally and spread the melted chocolate over the baked side of the bottom layer of sponge. Leave it to set firm. Line the clean cake tin with baking parchment or cling film and, when the chocolate has set, place the layer of sponge chocolate-side down in the tin.

Mix the remaining lemon juice with the 4 tablespoons of sugar syrup and the gin. Drizzle the bottom layer of sponge with a little of this syrup, then spread a third of the mousse over the sponge. Repeat with the other 2 layers of sponge and the remaining mousse. Level the surface and chill in the fridge for at least 4 hours, preferably overnight.

If using the jelly, melt it until it is just liquid. Leave it to cool until syrupy, then spoon it over the top of the mousse. Chill the mousse again for at least 1 hour.

Very carefully unmould the cake – the easiest way is to cover the surface with cling film, then turn it out on to a flat board. Invert the cake and peel off the cling film. Cut the cake into 16 squares and, if you wish, decorate the top with a little piped chocolate.

Sienna Cake with Honeycomb

60g (2oz) dried apricots, chopped

250g (8½oz) dried figs, chopped

200ml (7fl oz) grappa

200g (7oz) plain flour

1 tbsp cocoa powder

½ tsp ground cinnamon

100g (3½oz) flaked almonds, toasted

100g (3½oz) hazelnuts, toasted and chopped

100g (3½oz) unsalted butter

100g (3½oz) caster sugar

1 egg

150ml (¼ pint) clear honey

200g (7oz) natural honeycomb, cut into

1.5cm (½ inch) pieces

icing sugar for dusting

Soak the apricots and figs in the grappa overnight – or for several days in advance. Drain thoroughly and reserve the grappa.

Grease a 25cm (10 inch) shallow round cake tin and line with baking parchment or rice paper. Preheat the oven to 180°C/350°F/Gas Mark 4. Sift the flour, cocoa powder and cinnamon into a bowl and mix in the almonds, hazelnuts, apricots and figs. In a separate bowl, cream the butter and sugar until pale and fluffy, then beat in the egg.

In a heavy-based pan, bring the honey and reserved grappa to the boil, stirring frequently, then simmer gently for 7–8 minutes. Remove from the heat and cool slightly, then stir in the dry ingredients, the creamed mixture and the honeycomb. Transfer the mixture to the prepared tin and bake for 40–45 minutes, until firm to the touch. Leave to cool, then remove from the tin and peel off the baking parchment, is using. Dust generously with icing sugar before serving.

Chocolate Nirvana

250g (8½oz) Sweet Pastry (see page 37)

120g (4oz) unsalted butter

5 tbsp fresh strong black coffee, preferably espresso

60g (2oz) caster sugar

180g (6oz) good-quality plain chocolate, chopped

3 eggs, beaten

75g (2½oz) hazelnuts, toasted and ground

20g (¾oz) hazelnuts, toasted and cut into slivers

For the glaze

2 tbsp milk

1 tbsp double cream

20g (¾oz) caster sugar

120g (4oz) good-quality plain chocolate

On a lightly floured surface, roll out the pastry thinly and use to line a deep 20cm (8 inch) flan tin. Line the pastry case with greaseproof paper or kitchen foil and weight it down with baking beans. Rest it in the fridge for 20 minutes while you heat the oven to 190°C/375°F/Gas Mark 5. Bake the pastry case for approximately 15 minutes, then remove the paper and beans and bake for a further 5 minutes.

For the filling, melt the butter in a bowl set over a pan of simmering water. Add the coffee and sugar and stir until smooth. Add the chocolate to the bowl and stir occasionally until melted. Remove from the heat and beat in the eggs and ground hazelnuts until evenly mixed. Pour into the prepared pastry case and bake for about 25 minutes, until just firm to the touch. Leave to cool.

For the glaze, combine the milk, double cream, sugar and 1 tablespoon of water in a small saucepan and bring to the boil. Remove from the heat, add the chocolate and mix until melted and smooth. Pour the glaze over the tart and sprinkle the chopped hazelnuts around the edge. Leave to set firm.

SIENNA CAKE WITH HONEYCOMB (PAGE 115), CHOCOLATE NIRVANA (PAGE 115), MARSALA AND ALMOND CAKE,
AND TANGY LEMON MOUSSE SQUARES (PAGE 114)

Marsala and Almond Cake

4 tbsp Marsala
200ml (7fl oz) fresh orange juice
juice of 1 lemon
2 cloves
350g (12oz) caster sugar
150g (5oz) unsalted butter
3 eggs
1 tbsp glycerine
225g (8oz) plain flour, sifted
1 tsp baking powder
½ tsp cinnamon
45g (1½oz) good-quality plain
chocolate, grated
90g (3oz) ground almonds
60g (2oz) flaked almonds

Planning ahead: You can bake this cake at least two days in advance, and store it in an airtight tin.

Grease a 23cm (9 inch) round cake tin. Preheat the oven to 180°C/350°F/Gas Mark 4. Combine the Marsala, orange juice, lemon juice, cloves and half the sugar in a heavy-based saucepan. Boil until reduced by four-fifths and then leave to cool. Remove the cloves.

Cream the butter and remaining sugar until light and fluffy, then beat in the eggs one at a time. Beat in the glycerine. Fold in the sifted flour, baking powder, cinnamon, chocolate and ground almonds, then fold in the Marsala liquid. Transfer the mixture to the prepared tin, level the surface and sprinkle the flaked almonds on top. Bake for about 45 minutes, until risen and firm to the touch. Cool in the tin for a few minutes, then turn out on to a wire rack and leave to cool completely.

To Caramelize Orange or Grapefruit Zest

2 oranges or grapefruit
150g (5oz) caster sugar
100ml (3½fl oz) water
100ml (3½fl oz) grenadine (optional)

Pare the rind from the fruit and cut it into thin strips. Blanch in boiling water for 30 seconds, then drain. Combine the caster sugar with the water and grenadine, if using. Add the zest and simmer for about 10 minutes until the syrup is reduced by half. Leave to cool in the syrup. You can keep it like this in the fridge for 2–3 weeks.

To Caramelize Orange or Grapefruit Segments

orange or grapefruit segments
icing sugar

There are two ways of doing this: either dust the segments heavily with icing sugar and caramelize the sugar with a blow torch (used professionally because of its intense heat), or dip the segments in caramel and place them on baking parchment to set.

DINNER

There are people who confuse dinner with interior design. For them, the choice of china, flowers and table settings becomes more important than the meal itself. Sadder still are people who see dinner as a competitive event, an exercise in culinary one-upmanship.

Both these approaches seem to me to be missing the point. I am all for making sure the different elements of a successful dinner party complement each other – wine, table settings and the choice of guests are all are important – but food comes first.

People usually have more time at dinner than they do at lunch. Dinner is also the meal they look forward to most, so there's every reason to serve your guests something special, to try that bit harder and to invest a little extra time and care in the meal you are preparing. But that doesn't have to mean tracking down exotic ingredients or choosing dauntingly complicated recipes. Simple and tasty, well-balanced and attractively presented – that, for me, is a working definition of a good dinner menu.

I take a similar approach to wine. These days it is possible to buy wines of excellent quality that do not cost the earth. You are better off serving a consistent, if inexpensive, choice of wines throughout the meal than, for example, offering a cheap white followed by an expensive red.

Most important of all, never forget one simple truth – dinner is for pleasure! For old friends or family, new friends or business colleagues, dinner is the ideal opportunity to enjoy relaxed conversation, pleasant company and, best of all, good food.

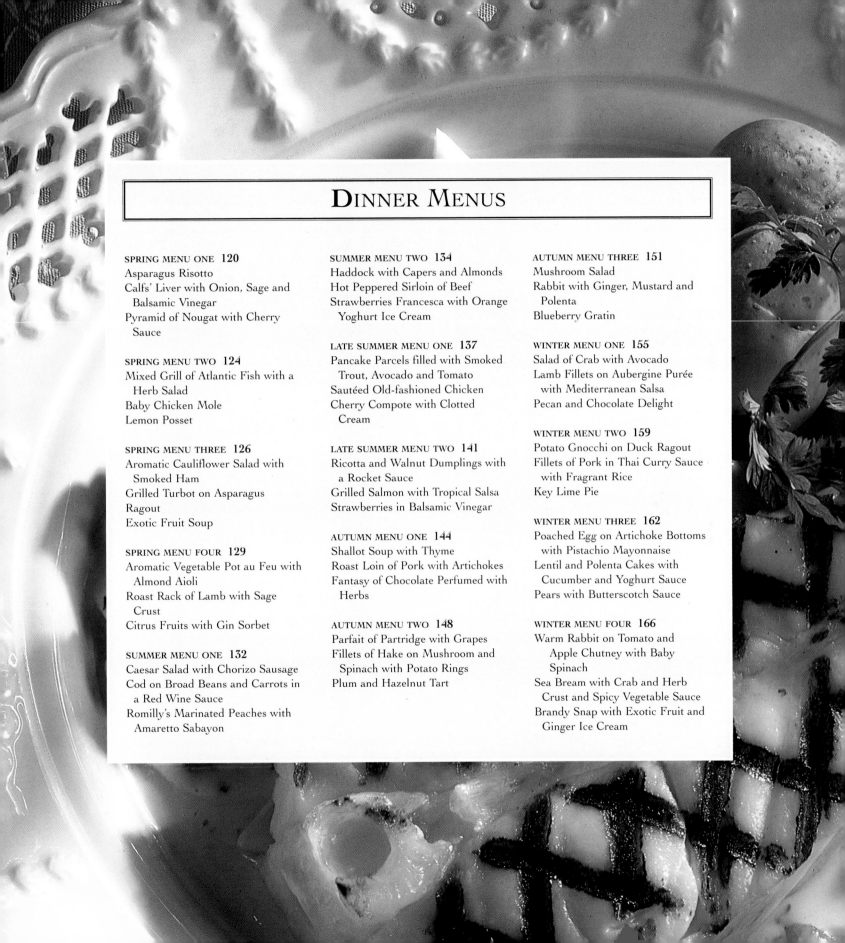

DINNER MENUS

SPRING MENU ONE 120
Asparagus Risotto
Calfs' Liver with Onion, Sage and
Balsamic Vinegar
Pyramid of Nougat with Cherry
Sauce

SPRING MENU TWO 124
Mixed Grill of Atlantic Fish with a
Herb Salad
Baby Chicken Mole
Lemon Posset

SPRING MENU THREE 126
Aromatic Cauliflower Salad with
Smoked Ham
Grilled Turbot on Asparagus
Ragout
Exotic Fruit Soup

SPRING MENU FOUR 129
Aromatic Vegetable Pot au Feu with
Almond Aioli
Roast Rack of Lamb with Sage
Crust
Citrus Fruits with Gin Sorbet

SUMMER MENU ONE 132
Caesar Salad with Chorizo Sausage
Cod on Broad Beans and Carrots in
a Red Wine Sauce
Romilly's Marinated Peaches with
Amaretto Sabayon

SUMMER MENU TWO 134
Haddock with Capers and Almonds
Hot Peppered Sirloin of Beef
Strawberries Francesca with Orange
Yoghurt Ice Cream

LATE SUMMER MENU ONE 137
Pancake Parcels filled with Smoked
Trout, Avocado and Tomato
Sautéed Old-fashioned Chicken
Cherry Compote with Clotted
Cream

LATE SUMMER MENU TWO 141
Ricotta and Walnut Dumplings with
a Rocket Sauce
Grilled Salmon with Tropical Salsa
Strawberries in Balsamic Vinegar

AUTUMN MENU ONE 144
Shallot Soup with Thyme
Roast Loin of Pork with Artichokes
Fantasy of Chocolate Perfumed with
Herbs

AUTUMN MENU TWO 148
Parfait of Partridge with Grapes
Fillets of Hake on Mushroom and
Spinach with Potato Rings
Plum and Hazelnut Tart

AUTUMN MENU THREE 151
Mushroom Salad
Rabbit with Ginger, Mustard and
Polenta
Blueberry Gratin

WINTER MENU ONE 155
Salad of Crab with Avocado
Lamb Fillets on Aubergine Purée
with Mediterranean Salsa
Pecan and Chocolate Delight

WINTER MENU TWO 159
Potato Gnocchi on Duck Ragout
Fillets of Pork in Thai Curry Sauce
with Fragrant Rice
Key Lime Pie

WINTER MENU THREE 162
Poached Egg on Artichoke Bottoms
with Pistachio Mayonnaise
Lentil and Polenta Cakes with
Cucumber and Yoghurt Sauce
Pears with Butterscotch Sauce

WINTER MENU FOUR 166
Warm Rabbit on Tomato and
Apple Chutney with Baby
Spinach
Sea Bream with Crab and Herb
Crust and Spicy Vegetable Sauce
Brandy Snap with Exotic Fruit and
Ginger Ice Cream

SPRING MENU ONE

ASPARAGUS RISOTTO
CALFS' LIVER WITH ONION, SAGE AND BALSAMIC VINEGAR
PYRAMID OF NOUGAT WITH CHERRY SAUCE

ASPARAGUS RISOTTO

20 medium-thick asparagus spears

900ml (1½ pints) chicken stock

2 tbsp olive oil

1 onion, peeled and finely chopped

½ clove of garlic, peeled and finely chopped

250g (8½oz) risotto rice

60g (2oz) unsalted butter

100ml (3½fl oz) dry white wine

30g (1oz) Parmesan cheese, freshly grated

shavings of Parmesan cheese and sprigs of
chervil to garnish

salt and peppermill

TIPS

When asparagus is in season, tender, young green spears need only the 'leaves' on the sides of the stalks removed with a knife or a vegetable peeler.

White asparagus, which is now available from the Continent, needs to be carefully peeled and the ends broken off, as they are often very woody. It should be very well cooked.

The flavour of white asparagus is somewhat more intense than the green.

At the Savoy I like to garnish dishes with both green and white asparagus, for their contrasting colours and flavours.

Planning ahead: To save time, peel and cook the asparagus a day in advance. You can also prepare the risotto in advance, up to the point when you add the chicken stock. Simmer for 5 minutes and then take it off the heat and leave to cool.

Peel the asparagus evenly and carefully, then tie into bundles of 10 and trim the ends to an even length. Cook in boiling salted water for 5–7 minutes, until just tender but still firm. Drain and refresh in iced water, then dry on a kitchen cloth.

Heat the chicken stock to simmering point. Heat the oil in a wide, heavy-based pan, add the onion and cook until soft and translucent; add the garlic and cook for a further minute. Add the rice and cook for about 30 seconds, stirring to coat the grains with the oil. Pour in just enough of the simmering chicken stock to cover the rice. Cook over a moderate heat, stirring frequently and adding more stock as it is absorbed so that the rice is always just covered by the liquid. The total cooking time should be about 20 minutes.

While the rice is cooking, cut the asparagus in half and reserve the tips; slice the stalks. Place the tips in a pan with 2 tablespoons of the chicken stock and a knob of the butter. Heat until the stock has evaporated and the asparagus is hot and glazed with the butter.

When the rice is just tender, stir in the sliced asparagus and the white wine. Cook for a further 20 seconds, remove from the heat and stir in the remaining butter and the grated Parmesan. Season with salt and pepper.

Spoon the risotto into shallow soup bowls and garnish with the asparagus tips, Parmesan cheese shavings and chervil.

CALFS' LIVER WITH ONION, SAGE AND BALSAMIC VINEGAR

3 tbsp olive oil

450g (1lb) calfs' liver, skin and gristle removed
(ask your butcher to do this) and cut into
6mm (¼ inch) strips

4 sage leaves, roughly chopped

1 onion, peeled and finely chopped

100ml (3½fl oz) dry white wine

4 tbsp balsamic vinegar

45g (1½oz) unsalted butter, chilled and cut
into cubes

TIP

Make sure that any membrane or nerves
on the liver are removed

Calfs' liver, sage and balsamic vinegar is a perfect combination. It goes well with creamed potatoes or potato purée made with garlic and olive oil.

Heat a non-stick pan and add 1 tablespoon of the olive oil and half the liver. Seal very quickly until browned on all sides, then add salt, pepper and half the sage leaves. Remove from the pan and keep warm. Cook the remaining liver in the same way.

Add the remaining oil to the pan and sweat the onion until soft and translucent. Add the white wine and boil fast until reduced by two-thirds. Stir in the balsamic vinegar and bring to the boil, then remove from the heat. Return the liver to the pan and whisk in the chilled butter a few pieces at a time. Adjust the seasoning. Do not allow to boil again or the liver will be tough.

PYRAMID OF NOUGAT WITH CHERRY SAUCE

PYRAMID OF NOUGAT WITH CHERRY SAUCE

6 egg yolks

100g (3½oz) icing sugar

50g (1¾oz) lavender honey

500ml (16fl oz) double cream, semi-whipped

30g (1oz) pine kernels, toasted

30g (1oz) pistachio nuts, blanched in milk,
then peeled

30g (1oz) candied peel, chopped

30g (1oz) glacé cherries, chopped

200g (7oz) Griottines cherries in Armagnac, or
other canned or bottled cherries

100ml (3½fl oz) sugar syrup (see page 109)

Planning ahead: This has to be prepared at least a day in advance.

Whisk the egg yolks with the icing sugar in a large bowl until thick and pale. Boil the honey in a small pan until it reaches 120°C/240°F on a sugar thermometer. Immediately pour it on to the yolks and sugar, whisking constantly with an electric hand mixer set on the highest speed. Continue to whisk until the mixture is cold, then fold in the semi-whipped cream. Fold in the pine kernels, pistachio nuts, candied peel and glacé cherries and freeze in moulds of your choice, such as dariole moulds or ramekins (in the picture it is frozen in pyramid moulds, hence the name).

Liquidize the Griottines cherries with the sugar syrup. To serve, dip the moulds very quickly in hot water and turn out on to plates. Pour the sauce around.

NOTE: In the picture the pyramid is covered by a chocolate spiral. This can only be achieved with tempered couverture chocolate, which is then piped in a spiral on to non-stick paper. Once set, the chocolate is still pliable.

TIPS

You can use other fruit and nuts or, indeed, liqueur in this parfait to achieve a different flavour.

Depending on the size of your moulds, this might be enough to serve 6–8.

SPRING MENU TWO

MIXED GRILL OF ATLANTIC FISH WITH A HERB SALAD
BABY CHICKEN MOLE
LEMON POSSET

MIXED GRILL OF ATLANTIC FISH WITH A HERB SALAD

4 king scallops (see method)

4 small baby sea bass fillets

4 small red mullet fillets

4 x 60g (2oz) salmon fillets, skinned

4 langoustine tails

150g (5oz) unsalted butter

3 shallots, peeled and finely chopped

100ml (3½fl oz) fish or chicken stock

4 tbsp white wine vinegar

100ml (3½fl oz) dry white wine

½ tsp white peppercorns, crushed

1 star anise, crushed (optional)

2 tbsp groundnut oil

4 tbsp double cream

keta caviar to garnish (optional)

sea salt flakes and cayenne pepper

For the herb salad

1 tbsp vinegar

1 tbsp lime juice

2 tbsp extra virgin olive oil

15g (½oz) bunch of chervil

15g (½oz) chives, cut into 1.5cm (½ inch) lengths

10g (¼oz) bunch of basil

a few sprigs of dill

50g (1¾oz) celery leaves, chopped

20g (¾oz) rocket

salt and peppermill

All the fish will need different cooking times depending on their thickness, so take care. The salmon is likely to take slightly longer than the sea bass and mullet, the scallops and langoustines slightly less time. Allow about 5 minutes in all.

Ask your fishmonger to remove the scallops from their shells and to clean them. Remove the tiny bones from the fish fillets with tweezers.

For the salad, mix the vinegar and lime juice with the olive oil and season well with salt and pepper.

Melt 15g (½oz) of the butter in a heavy-based saucepan, add the shallots and cook gently until soft and nearly translucent, stirring frequently. Stir in the stock, wine vinegar, wine, peppercorns and star anise, if using. Bring to the boil and boil fast until the liquid is reduced by three-quarters. Remove from the heat and leave to cool for a few minutes.

Season all the fish and shellfish with sea salt flakes, turn them in the groundnut oil and cook under a preheated grill. Test with a knife; when cooked they should be translucent and moist inside.

Cut the remaining butter into small cubes. Return the sauce to a very low heat and gradually whisk in the rest of the butter, a few pieces at a time. If the sauce becomes too thick, add a little more stock. Strain the sauce through a fine sieve into a clean saucepan, pressing down on the shallots and seasonings in the sieve to extract maximum liquid and flavour. Season with salt and cayenne pepper, then stir in the cream. If necessary, set the pan in a larger pan of gently simmering water to keep it warm until serving; do not allow the sauce to boil.

Toss all the herbs in the dressing and adjust the seasoning. Arrange the fish around the edges of warmed serving plates, place a handful of the herb salad in the centre of each one and pour a little of the butter sauce between the fillets of fish. Garnish with keta caviar, if wished.

Baby Chicken Mole

4 baby chickens (poussins) (see method)

1 onion, peeled and chopped

3 tbsp olive oil

2 cloves of garlic, crushed

2 tbsp unsweetened cocoa powder

1 tbsp tomato purée

2 tbsp ground cumin

1 tsp ground cinnamon

1 tsp ground coriander

½ tsp cayenne pepper

75g (2½oz) roasted peanuts

500ml (16fl oz) chicken stock

100ml (3½fl oz) dry white wine

coriander leaves to garnish

salt and peppermill

TIP

If you prefer, take the chickens out of the sauce and remove their rib cages, which makes them easier to deal with on the plate. Return them to the sauce to serve.

Over the years, many chefs from all over the world have come to work with us at the Savoy, and during their last few days I usually ask them to cook a traditional dish from their own country. Baby Chicken Mole was cooked for us by Cynthia Bloebaum, from San Francisco. When she told me that she wanted to cook chicken in cocoa sauce, I had my doubts. However, I have to say that it was absolutely delicious.

Ask your butcher to split the chickens from the back, removing the back bone and flatten them (often referred to as butterflied or spatchcocked).

In a small pan, sauté the onion in 1 tablespoon of the olive oil until translucent. Add the crushed garlic and cook for a further minute. Stir in the cocoa powder, tomato purée, spices and peanuts and mix thoroughly. Add the chicken stock, bring to the boil and simmer, uncovered, until reduced by half – this will take at least 20 minutes. Leave to cool.

While the sauce is cooking, prepare the chickens. Season them with salt and pepper, then heat the remaining olive oil in a large pan and brown the chickens in it on both sides. Remove from the pan and drain on kitchen paper. Pour off the oil from the pan, pour in the white wine and stir to deglaze, softening any sediment. Return the chickens to the pan. Purée the sauce and pour it over the chickens. Bring to the boil, then cover and simmer until the chickens are tender, about 30 minutes. Adjust the seasoning and garnish with fresh coriander

Lemon Posset

600ml (1 pint) double cream

finely grated zest and juice of 2 lemons

150g (5oz) caster sugar

2–3 tbsp good brandy

100g (3½oz) ratafias

This is a good example of simple food achieving a great impact.

Planning ahead: Prepare this dish a day in advance.

Combine the cream, lemon zest and sugar in a saucepan and bring just to simmering point. Remove from the heat and leave to cool, stirring occasionally to prevent a skin forming. When almost cool, stir in the lemon juice and brandy. Arrange the ratafias in a bowl or individual glasses and pour over the lemon cream. Cover and chill overnight in the fridge.

SPRING MENU THREE

AROMATIC CAULIFLOWER SALAD WITH SMOKED HAM
GRILLED TURBOT ON ASPARAGUS RAGOUT
EXOTIC FRUIT SOUP

AROMATIC CAULIFLOWER SALAD WITH SMOKED HAM

6 tbsp olive oil

450g (1lb) cauliflower florets (about 1 large cauliflower)

2 carrots, peeled and thinly sliced

3 tbsp dry white wine

4 tbsp white wine vinegar

1 tbsp sugar

1 star anise

½ bay leaf

½ tsp black peppercorns, crushed

60g (2oz) broad beans, blanched and skinned

12 thin slices of smoked ham

salt and peppermill

In place of ham you can use any smoked meat, such as duck breast, goose breast, quail or venison. If you do use ham, why not try some of the English ones, which compare very well with the French and Italian.

Planning ahead: The cauliflower salad can be prepared up to 24 hours in advance.

Heat half the oil in a flameproof casserole over a low heat, add the cauliflower and carrots and season with salt and pepper. Add the wine, vinegar and sugar and cook until reduced to a glaze, stirring frequently. Pour in enough water just to cover the vegetables, then add the star anise, bay leaf and black peppercorns and cover with a lid. Simmer for about 6 minutes, until the vegetables are tender but still firm. Remove from the heat, add the broad beans and leave to cool completely.

Remove the vegetables from the cooking liquid and boil it fast to reduce it by three-quarters. Leave to cool. Stir the remaining oil into the liquid, toss the vegetables in it and season to taste.

To serve, place the vegetables on plates and arrange the slices of ham around them.

AROMATIC CAULIFLOWER SALAD WITH SMOKED HAM, GRILLED TURBOT ON ASPARAGUS RAGOUT, AND
EXOTIC FRUIT SOUP

GRILLED TURBOT ON ASPARAGUS RAGOUT

4 x 250g (8½oz) pieces of turbot on the bone

4 tbsp groundnut oil

16 large asparagus spears, peeled

30g (1oz) butter

1 tbsp plain flour

100ml (3½fl oz) dry white wine

100ml (3½fl oz) double cream

2 plum tomatoes, blanched, peeled, deseeded and diced

1 tbsp chopped chervil

chervil to garnish

salt and peppermill

TIP

Always refresh asparagus in iced water because it prevents them cooking further and they also retain their colour.

Heat the oven to 220°C/425°F/Gas Mark 7. Wash and dry the turbot well, season with salt and pepper and turn it in the oil to coat.

Tie the asparagus spears into bundles of 8 and trim the ends so they are all the same length. Boil in 1.5 litres (2½ pints) of salted water for 5–7 minutes, until *al dente*, remove from the pan and refresh in iced water. Boil 300ml (½ pint) of the asparagus cooking water to reduce by two-thirds.

Melt the butter in a heavy-based saucepan, stir in the flour and cook for 2 minutes without letting it colour, stirring constantly. Remove from the heat, then gradually add the hot asparagus stock and the white wine, stirring all the time. Return to the heat and cook gently until the sauce is thick enough to coat the back of a spoon. Simmer for 2 minutes, then add the cream and simmer for a further minute. Season with salt and pepper and pass through a fine sieve.

Brown the turbot on both sides in a ridged pan or in a frying pan, then transfer to the oven and bake for about 12 minutes. Check the fish by inserting a knife next to the bone; the flesh should be slightly translucent.

Meanwhile, cut the asparagus spears in half, reheat them in the sauce, then stir in the tomato and chervil. Spoon the asparagus ragout into large soup plates. Skin the turbot, place the fish on top of the asparagus and garnish with chervil. Serve with Jersey new potatoes, boiled in their skins.

EXOTIC FRUIT SOUP

400ml (14fl oz) water

200g (7oz) caster sugar

½ vanilla pod, split

½ tsp freshly grated ginger

½ tsp chopped mint (reserve the stalk)

finely grated zest of ½ lemon

6 passion fruit

an assortment of soft fruit in season

1 very ripe small mango, peeled, stoned and cut into cubes

8 strawberries, quartered

1 small melon, cut into cubes

This soup is refreshing and clears the palate.

Planning ahead: Prepare the syrup a day in advance. You can also cut the fruit up to 1 hour before, cover it with cling film and keep in the fridge.

Put the water, sugar, vanilla pod, ginger and mint stalk in a heavy-based saucepan and bring to the boil. Add the lemon zest. When the sugar has dissolved, remove from the heat and leave to cool.

Strain the sugar syrup through a fine sieve. Cut the passion fruit in half and add the seeds to the syrup, together with the chopped mint. Prepare the seasonal fruit as necessary and divide all the fruit between 4 bowls. Pour on the syrup.

Spring Menu Four

Aromatic Vegetable Pot au Feu with Almond Aioli
Roast Rack of Lamb with Sage Crust
Citrus Fruits with Gin Sorbet

Aromatic Vegetable Pot au Feu with Almond Aioli

2 onions, peeled and finely chopped

2 tbsp groundnut oil

2 small fennel bulbs, trimmed and quartered

3 celery sticks, trimmed and quartered

200g (7oz) carrots, peeled and quartered

200g (7oz) celeriac, peeled and cut into 2cm
(¾ inch) cubes

3 medium leeks, trimmed, cut lengthways in
half, then sliced 1cm (⅓ inch) thick

4 cloves of garlic, peeled

8 button onions, peeled

200ml (7fl oz) dry white wine

500ml (16fl oz) water

2 star anise

½ tsp black peppercorns

½ tsp coriander seeds

1 small bay leaf

8 asparagus spears, peeled and cut in half

8 slices of French bread, cut 6mm (¼ inch)
thick and toasted

salt and peppermill

For the Aioli – makes 300ml (½ pint)

3 cloves of garlic, peeled

½ tsp salt

50g (1¾oz) ground almonds

3 tbsp white wine vinegar or lemon juice

2 egg yolks

250ml (8fl oz) olive oil

This can be served as a vegetable course or a starter.

Planning ahead: Prepare this in advance up to the stage where the asparagus is added.

Sweat the onions in the oil until soft and translucent. Add all the other vegetables except the asparagus, then pour in the white wine and water and season with salt and pepper.

Crush the star anise and tie them in a piece of muslin with the peppercorns, coriander seeds and bay leaf. Add to the vegetables, then cover and simmer gently for 20 minutes, skimming occasionally. Add the asparagus and simmer for a further 7–8 minutes, until the vegetables are *al dente*. Adjust seasoning. Serve with the toasted French bread and the aioli.

To make the almond aioli, thoroughly crush the garlic with the salt in a pestle and mortar. Mix in the ground almonds, vinegar or lemon juice and egg yolks. Using a wooden spoon or an electric hand mixer, incorporate the olive oil drop by drop until the mixture has a thick, mayonnaise-type consistency. When the sauce begins to thicken and looks like soft butter it is ready.

ROAST RACK OF LAMB WITH SAGE CRUST

4 tbsp groundnut oil

2 racks of lamb (ask your butcher for

450g/1lb bones and trimmings, too)

1 small fennel bulb, cut into small cubes

(reserve the feathery tops)

4 spring onions, diced

45g (1½oz) celery, diced

2 cloves of garlic, peeled and crushed

4 tbsp dry white wine

400ml (14fl oz) chicken stock

1 tsp black peppercorns

15g (½oz) bunch of sage, leaves chopped

(reserve the stalks)

15g (½oz) bunch of flat-leaf parsley, leaves

chopped (reserve the stalks)

2 shallots, peeled and chopped

75g (2½oz) fresh breadcrumbs

1 tbsp plain flour

1 egg, beaten

½ tbsp Pernod

50g (1¾oz) unsalted butter, chilled and cut

into cubes

salt and peppermill

Lamb simply shouts out for herbs! The herb crust is not a new idea but sage is slightly unusual and the result is a true surprise.

Preheat the oven to maximum. On the hob, heat 2 tablespoons of the oil in a roasting tin, then add the bones and meat trimmings and brown well. Transfer to the oven and roast for 10 minutes, until golden brown. Add the fennel, spring onions, celery and half the garlic and roast for a further 5 minutes. Put the roasting tin back on the hob and stir in the white wine and chicken stock. Add the peppercorns and the sage and parsley stalks, then cover with foil or a baking tray and simmer gently for about 30 minutes, stirring and skimming frequently. Pour through a fine sieve into a clean pan and boil until reduced to 200ml (7fl oz).

Season the racks of lamb with salt and pepper. Reduce the oven temperature to 190°C/375°F/Gas Mark 5 and roast the lamb for 12 minutes on each side. Sweat the shallots in the remaining oil until translucent, then add the breadcrumbs, remaining garlic, sage and parsley leaves and fennel tops and season with salt and pepper. Remove the lamb from the roasting tin and leave to cool for 5 minutes.

Dip the fat side of the lamb in the flour, then into the egg, and finally cover it well with the herb and breadcrumb mixture, pressing it on firmly. Return the lamb to the roasting tin so that the meat is resting on the bones and roast for a further 8 minutes until medium cooked, basting frequently. The sage crust should be crisp and brown; crisp it up under the grill, if necessary.

Remove the meat from the tin and leave to rest for 10 minutes in a warm place. Pour away the fat from the roasting tin and pour in the Pernod and the reduced stock mixture. Simmer for a minute, then whisk in the cold butter a few pieces at a time. Adjust the seasoning. Cut the lamb carefully between the bones and serve the sauce on the side.

TIP

If you don't have any lamb bones and trimmings, simply reduce the chicken stock by half to concentrate the flavour.

CITRUS FRUITS WITH GIN SORBET

2 oranges

2 limes

2 blood oranges

2 pink grapefruit

4 tbsp orange blossom honey

For the sorbet

250ml (8fl oz) lemon juice

100g (3½oz) caster sugar

300ml (½ pint) water

5 tbsp gin

TIPS

This is a very light dessert which cleans the palate. It could be used as an intermediate course between starter and main course during the summer.

If the sorbet is left in the freezer and has frozen very hard, transfer it to the fridge 20-30 minutes before serving so that it can soften slightly.

Planning ahead: The sorbet can be made at least a day in advance. You can also prepare the orange zest, and marinate the fruit.

Caramelize the zest from the two oranges, as described on page 117, preferably using the grenadine.

Peel and segment all the fruit, carefully removing all the pips, pith and membrane.

Warm the honey and pour it over the fruit. Cover and leave to marinate in a cool place for at least 6 hours or overnight.

For the sorbet, put the lemon juice, sugar, water and gin in a saucepan and heat until the sugar dissolves, then bring to the boil. Leave to cool. Pass through a fine sieve and freeze in an ice-cream machine according to the manufacturer's instructions. Alternatively, pour the mixture into a freezerproof container, cover and freeze until almost set. Transfer to a food processor and whizz until broken up and well mixed. Return to the container and freeze again. For a finer-textured sorbet, repeat this process once more. Freeze until firm. Just before serving, mix the gin sorbet well with a fork and, if it is too hard, place it in the fridge for 20 minutes to soften slightly.

Arrange the citrus fruit in shallow bowls, pour over a little of the juice and sprinkle with the orange zest. Use 2 tablespoons to shape quenelles of sorbet and place one on each portion of fruit.

SUMMER MENU ONE

CAESAR SALAD WITH CHORIZO SAUSAGE
COD ON BROAD BEANS AND CARROTS IN A RED WINE SAUCE
ROMILLY'S MARINATED PEACHES WITH AMARETTO SABAYON

CAESAR SALAD WITH CHORIZO SAUSAGE

4 slices of white bread, crusts removed
2 Cos lettuces, cut into 5cm (2 inch) pieces
30g (1oz) Parmesan cheese, freshly grated
1 chorizo sausage, cut into slices
6mm (¼ inch) thick

For the dressing
3 egg yolks
1 clove of garlic, peeled and crushed
2 anchovy fillets
2 tbsp chopped shallots
1 tsp English mustard
1 tsp Worcestershire sauce
2 tbsp balsamic vinegar
½ small red chilli, deseeded and chopped
100ml (3½fl oz) olive oil
salt and peppermill

This is my own version of Caesar salad dressing and it can be used for other crisp lettuces, such as Webb's Wonder or Little Gem. You could also substitute small fish cakes or warm goats' cheese or even small pieces of grilled fish for the chorizo sausage.

Preheat the oven to 190°C/375°F/Gas Mark 5. Cut the bread into 1cm (⅓ inch) squares, place on a baking tray and toast in the oven for about 20 minutes, until crisp and golden, turning occasionally. Leave to cool (they can be made in advance and stored in an airtight container).

To make the dressing, place the egg yolks, garlic, anchovy fillets, shallots, mustard, Worcestershire sauce, balsamic vinegar and chilli in a liquidizer. With the motor running, add the olive oil very slowly until it forms a thick sauce. Season to taste with salt and pepper.

Mix the lettuce and Parmesan cheese together in a bowl, add the dressing and toss well. The leaves should be just coated with the dressing. Adjust the seasoning, then transfer the salad to deep soup plates, garnish with the sausage and sprinkle with the croutons.

COD ON BROAD BEANS AND CARROTS IN A RED WINE SAUCE

1 shallot, peeled and finely chopped

½ tsp black peppercorns, crushed

400ml (14fl oz) fish or chicken stock

400ml (14fl oz) full-bodied red wine

1 clove of garlic, peeled

1 sprig of thyme

4 tbsp double cream

½ tsp redcurrant jelly

150g (5oz) unsalted butter, chilled and cut into cubes

4 x 140g (4½oz) cod fillets, bones and skin removed

1 tbsp vegetable oil

4 new carrots, thinly sliced

100g (3½oz) broad beans, blanched and skinned

salt and peppermill

Preheat the oven to 200°C/400°F/Gas Mark 6. Place the shallot, peppercorns and stock in a heavy-based pan and boil fast until reduced to a glaze. Add the red wine, garlic and thyme and boil until reduced by about a fifth. Add the cream and redcurrant jelly and reduce again until the sauce thickens slightly. Remove from the heat and whisk in all but a small knob of the butter, a few pieces at a time. Season with salt and pepper and pass through a fine sieve. Keep the sauce warm in a bain-marie but do not allow it to boil again.

Dry the cod fillets on kitchen paper and then season them. In a non-stick pan, fry the cod very quickly in the vegetable oil for 1 minute per side, until nicely coloured. Transfer to a baking tray and cook in the oven for 3–5 minutes, depending on the thickness of the fillets. Test with a knife; the fish should be translucent in the centre.

Steam the carrots until *al dente*, adding the broad beans at the last minute to heat through. Toss the carrots and broad beans in the remaining butter and season lightly. Divide the vegetables between 4 serving plates, set a piece of cod on top and pour the sauce around.

ROMILLY'S MARINATED PEACHES WITH AMARETTO SABAYON

6 ripe peaches

juice of ½ lemon

600ml (1 pint) red wine

½ cinnamon stick

1 clove

45g (1½oz) caster sugar

1 tsp cornflour

4 sprigs of mint to decorate

For the sabayon

3 egg yolks

3 tbsp Amaretto liqueur

45g (1½oz) caster sugar

2 tbsp orange juice

2 tbsp lemon juice

Put the peaches in a large saucepan of simmering water for 1 minute, then remove and place in a bowl of cold water with the lemon juice for 1 minute, or until cool enough to handle. Skin, halve and remove the stones.

Heat the red wine with the cinnamon stick, clove and sugar and boil fast until reduced by a third. Remove from the heat, add the peach halves and infuse for 5 minutes. Remove the peaches from the pan with a slotted spoon and bring the red wine syrup back to the boil. Mix the cornflour to a smooth paste with a little cold water. Stir it into the syrup and simmer for 5 minutes. Pour the syrup over the peaches and keep warm.

For the sabayon, place the egg yolks, liqueur, sugar and orange and lemon juices in a bowl set over a pan of simmering water and whisk with a hand-held electric mixer until it increases to about three times its original volume and develops a light, fluffy, mousse-like consistency.

Place 3 peach halves in each deep soup plate, pour some wine syrup over them and a generous helping of sabayon. Decorate with the mint.

SUMMER MENU TWO

HADDOCK WITH CAPERS AND ALMONDS
HOT PEPPERED SIRLOIN OF BEEF WITH TARRAGON AND CAPER SAUCE
STRAWBERRIES FRANCESCA WITH ORANGE YOGHURT ICE CREAM

HADDOCK WITH CAPERS AND ALMONDS

2 tbsp flaked almonds

4 x 120–150g (4–5oz) haddock fillets, skin
and bones removed

3 tbsp groundnut oil

2 heads of chicory

pinch of sugar

a little lemon juice to taste

60g (2oz) unsalted butter

½ tbsp white wine vinegar

1 tbsp capers

2 tbsp balsamic vinegar

salt and peppermill

Haddock is a local fish but it is undervalued in this country. Its delicate texture and flavour are also ideal for poaching and sautéeing.

Heat the oven to 200°C/400°F/Gas Mark 6. Toast the almonds in the oven for about 10 minutes or until golden, tossing occasionally so they colour evenly.

Wash and dry the haddock. Season with salt and pepper and fry quickly in 2 tablespoons of the groundnut oil until well coloured. Transfer to a buttered baking tray and cook in the oven for about 5 minutes, until just firm. Test by inserting a knife – the flesh should be translucent.

Remove the large outside leaves from the chicory and select about 6 medium leaves per person. Heat the remaining oil in a heavy-based pan, add the chicory and cook gently for 1–2 minutes, until warmed through. Turn over and season with a little salt and pepper, plus sugar and lemon juice to taste. Arrange the chicory in a fan shape on each plate and place the haddock at the side.

Slowly heat the butter in a pan until it turns a nutty brown colour. Remove from the heat and stir in the white wine vinegar, capers and a little salt. Pour this over the fish, sprinkle with the flaked almonds and then pour the balsamic vinegar over it.

HOT PEPPERED SIRLOIN OF BEEF WITH TARRAGON AND CAPER SAUCE

about 900g (2lb) sirloin of beef (1 rib), off the
bone and all fat removed

1 tbsp sea salt

1 tbsp English mustard

2 tbsp black peppercorns, finely crushed

2 tbsp vegetable oil

For the sauce

1 egg yolk

4 tbsp crème fraîche or double cream

1 tbsp white wine vinegar

1 tsp Dijon mustard

Worcestershire sauce

Tabasco sauce

100ml (3½fl oz) olive oil

2 tbsp chopped tarragon

1 tbsp capers

2 tbsp finely chopped spring onions

salt and peppermill

Planning ahead: The beef can be roasted well in advance and it can be eaten hot or cold. If you eat it cold, do not put it in the fridge as this will destroy the flavours.

Season the beef with the sea salt and brush on the mustard, then press on the peppercorns in an even coating. Preheat the oven to 200°C/400°F/Gas Mark 6.

Heat the vegetable oil in a roasting tin on the hob and brown the beef until sealed on all sides. Transfer to the oven and roast for about 20 minutes, until medium cooked. Remove from the tin and leave to rest in a cool place for about 40 minutes, until lukewarm. Collect the juices that run out of the meat during the resting time and pass them through a fine sieve.

While the meat is resting, prepare the sauce. In a food processor or liquidizer, mix the egg yolk, crème fraîche or cream, vinegar and Dijon mustard with a few drops of Worcestershire and Tabasco sauce and season with salt and pepper. With the machine running, add the olive oil in a trickle until the sauce has thickened. Transfer to a clean bowl and stir in the sieved meat juices, tarragon, capers and spring onions. Adjust the seasoning. Slice the beef thinly and serve with the sauce.

STRAWBERRIES FRANCESCA WITH ORANGE YOGHURT ICE CREAM

2 egg whites

100g (3½oz) caster sugar

200g (7oz) strawberries, hulled and quartered

For the ice cream

250ml (8fl oz) freshly squeezed orange juice

finely grated zest of 2 oranges

2 egg yolks

100g (3½oz) caster sugar

120ml (4fl oz) natural yoghurt

120ml (4fl oz) crème fraîche

One of the best investments you can make in your kitchen is an ice-cream machine. It enables you to make ice cream in hardly any time at all and the quality will be far superior to shop-bought ice cream.
You can prepare this dessert with any other summer fruit or indeed with exotic fruits. Should you wish, you can serve it with a fruit coulis such as strawberry or mango (see pages 57 and 168).

Planning ahead: You can make the ice cream at least 1 day ahead.

Put the orange juice and zest in a small saucepan and boil until reduced to 150ml (¼ pint). Whisk the egg yolks and sugar together until thick and pale, then pour on the reduced orange juice, whisking constantly. Return to the pan and cook over a gentle heat, stirring all the time, until thick enough to coat the back of the spoon. Remove from the heat and leave to cool, then whisk in the yoghurt and crème fraîche. Pass through a fine sieve. Freeze the mixture in an ice-cream machine according to the manufacturer's instructions. Alternatively, pour it into a large freezerproof bowl, cover and freeze until almost set. Transfer to a food processor and whisk until it is creamy and all the ice crystals have broken down. Return the mixture to the bowl, cover and place in the freezer again. Repeat this process twice, then freeze the ice cream until firm.

Just before serving, whisk the egg whites until stiff, then whisk in the sugar a spoonful at a time until the mixture is thick and glossy. Using a piping bag fitted with a 2cm (¾ inch) nozzle, pipe a border of meringue around the inside edge of 4 heatproof plates. Brown under a very hot grill for a minute or so. Spoon the strawberries into the centre of the meringue rings and place a ball of ice cream on top of the strawberries.

LATE SUMMER MENU ONE

PANCAKE PARCELS FILLED WITH SMOKED TROUT, AVOCADO AND TOMATO
SAUTÉED OLD-FASHIONED CHICKEN
CHERRY COMPOTE WITH CLOTTED CREAM

PANCAKE PARCELS FILLED WITH SMOKED TROUT, AVOCADO AND TOMATO

90g (3oz) small smoked trout fillets, skin and
bones removed

2 plum tomatoes, blanched, peeled,
deseeded and diced

30g (1oz) cucumber, peeled, deseeded and
finely diced

1 avocado, peeled, stoned and finely diced

a little lemon juice to taste

8 very long chives

4 eggs

2 tbsp chopped herbs, such as tarragon
and parsley

20g (¾oz) unsalted butter

For the sauce

100ml (3½fl oz) mayonnaise

2 tbsp tomato ketchup

1½ tbsp freshly grated horseradish

2 tbsp orange juice

2 tbsp yoghurt

1 tsp brandy

a little chicken or vegetable stock

2 tbsp chopped chives

salt and peppermill

This is an extremely light and summery recipe.

Planning ahead: Prepare the pancakes and filling in advance. It then takes 5 minutes to put together.

For the sauce, mix the mayonnaise, tomato ketchup, horseradish, orange juice, yoghurt and brandy and season with a little salt and pepper. Thin to a pouring consistency with chicken or vegetable stock. Stir in the chopped chives.

Flake the smoked trout fillets into small pieces and mix with the tomatoes, cucumber and avocado. Season with salt, pepper and a little lemon juice.

Blanch the chives in boiling water for 10 seconds, then refresh in iced water. Beat the eggs with the herbs and salt and pepper. Heat a little knob of butter in a 20cm (8 inch) non-stick omelette pan and use an eighth of the egg mixture to make a thin pancake. Repeat to make 7 more pancakes.

Place some of the smoked trout mixture in the centre of each pancake, then pull up the sides and use a chive to tie each one into a 'money bag'. Pour a little sauce on to each serving plate and arrange 2 pancakes on top.

SAUTÉED OLD-FASHIONED CHICKEN

2 x 1 kg (2¼lb) chickens (see method)

3 tbsp groundnut oil

120g (4oz) onions, peeled and finely
chopped

2 cloves of garlic, peeled and crushed

200g (7oz) plum tomatoes, blanched, peeled,
deseeded and diced

120ml (4fl oz) red wine vinegar

400ml (14fl oz) chicken stock

12 button onions

75g (2½oz) unsalted butter, chilled and cut
into cubes

2 tbsp chopped flat-leaf parsley

12 Pan-fried Garlic Cloves (see page 23)

salt and peppermill

From the age of three our middle daughter, Diana, refused to eat anything other than chicken, so we had a lot of it. This recipe seemed to go down extremely well, and my wife and I surprisingly still enjoy a nice chicken. The button onions have a sensational flavour when cooked in this way, and they are perfect for garnishing other dishes, too.

Ask your butcher to joint the chickens so that you have 4 drumsticks, 4 thighs, and 4 breast portions with a single wing section attached. If wished, remove the meat from the wing tip.

Heat the oven to 200°C/400°F/Gas Mark 6. Season the chicken with salt and pepper. Heat half the oil in a heavy flameproof casserole and brown the chicken pieces thoroughly on all sides. Remove from the pan, put the onions in the pan and sweat until soft. Add the garlic and sweat for a further minute. Add the tomatoes and cook until reduced down to a rough pulp, then add the vinegar and cook until completely evaporated. Return the chicken to the pan and add the stock. Bring to the boil, add salt and pepper, then cover and transfer to the oven. Cook for approximately 20 minutes, until tender.

Heat a small, heavy-based casserole, add the remaining oil and the button onions; they should fit in a single layer. Sauté them very quickly to colour them evenly, then season with salt and pepper, cover with a lid and transfer to the oven. Cook for about 15 minutes until tender but still firm.

Remove the chicken from the pan and keep warm. Boil the stock fast until reduced by half, then adjust the seasoning. Whisk in the butter a few pieces at a time and add half the parsley. Pour the sauce over the chicken, sprinkle with the remaining parsley and garnish with the button onions and pan-fried garlic.

SAUTÉED OLD-FASHIONED CHICKEN

CHERRY COMPOTE WITH CLOTTED CREAM

1 orange

50g (1¾oz) caster sugar

200ml (7fl oz) water

300g (10oz) ripe cherries, stoned

1 cinnamon stick

2 tbsp kirsch

2 tsp cornflour

1 tub of clotted cream

The cherry season in this country does not last very long and you should take full advantage of it, as cherries are undoubtedly one of nature's great treats. You can use ice cream instead of clotted cream if you prefer.

Planning ahead: This can be made in advance but be careful not to boil the cherries for too long.

Pare the zest from the orange in long strips. Put the sugar and water in a pan and bring to the boil. Add the cherries, orange zest, cinnamon and kirsch and bring back to the boil.

Mix the cornflour to a smooth paste with a little cold water. Stir into the cherry compote and cook, stirring, for a few minutes until lightly thickened. Leave to cool, then remove the orange zest and cinnamon stick. Spoon into bowls and serve with the clotted cream.

LATE SUMMER MENU TWO

RICOTTA AND WALNUT DUMPLINGS WIH A ROCKET SAUCE
GRILLED SALMON WITH TROPICAL SALSA
STRAWBERRIES IN BALSAMIC VINEGAR

RICOTTA AND WALNUT DUMPLINGS WITH A ROCKET SAUCE

600g (1¼lb) ricotta cheese

1 egg

60g (2oz) walnuts, toasted and chopped

60g (2oz) pecorino cheese, freshly grated

about 75g (2½oz) plain flour

2 tbsp groundnut oil

45g (1½oz) butter

50g (1¾oz) onion, finely chopped

1 clove of garlic, peeled and crushed

100ml (3½fl oz) dry white wine

200ml (7fl oz) double cream

200ml (7fl oz) chicken or vegetable stock

60g (2oz) rocket, chopped

2 tbsp chopped basil

chervil to garnish

salt and peppermill

This is a very popular vegetarian dish at the Savoy. At home, our daughter Diana suffers from many food allergies (she is also known as Allergy Annie), amongst them the very common one of allergy to dairy produce. So we use goats' milk ricotta, chicken stock instead of cream and dairy-free margarine instead of butter to make this delightful dish. Pecorino is a sheeps' milk cheese.

Planning ahead: You can cook the dumplings a few hours in advance and keep them under a damp cloth.

Drain the ricotta thoroughly, mix with the egg and season generously with salt and pepper. Add the walnuts and two-thirds of the pecorino, then gradually mix in the flour to make a soft but dry mixture. If the ricotta is very moist it might take more flour, or if it is very dry it might need less.

Turn the mixture on to a floured surface and roll out into sausage shapes about 2.5cm (1 inch) thick. Cut into 2cm (¾ inch) lengths and simmer in a large pan of boiling salted water for about 2 minutes – when the dumplings float to the surface they are ready. Refresh in iced water and leave under a damp cloth.

Put half the oil and half the butter in a pan and sweat the onion until translucent. Add the garlic and sweat for a further minute. Add the white wine and boil fast until reduced by half. Pour in the cream and stock and reduce again by half. Stir in the rocket and basil, simmer for 1 minute and then liquidize the sauce until it is smooth and evenly green. Adjust the seasoning and reheat gently.

Heat the remaining oil and butter in a non-stick pan and fry the dumplings on both sides until golden brown. Remove from the pan, sprinkle with the remaining pecorino and place briefly under a hot grill to brown the cheese. Pour a little sauce on to each serving plate, arrange the dumplings on top and garnish with chervil.

RICOTTA AND WALNUT DUMPLINGS WITH A ROCKET SAUCE, GRILLED SALMON WITH TROPICAL SALSA, AND
STRAWBERRIES IN BALSAMIC VINEGAR

GRILLED SALMON WITH TROPICAL SALSA

½ small pineapple, peeled and cored

½ pawpaw, peeled and deseeded

½ mango, peeled and stone removed

4 x 150g (5oz) salmon fillets, bones and
skin removed

1 tbsp groundnut oil

½ red onion, peeled and finely diced

1 plum tomato, blanched, peeled and diced

2 red chillies, deseeded and finely chopped

juice of 1 lime

2 tbsp finely chopped mint

salt and peppermill

TIP

Make sure that all the brown fatty bits are
removed from the salmon.

**Wild salmon is in season from March to August and is a delightful fish. The
farmed variety is quite acceptable and more easily available.
Make sure that the fruit for the salsa is ripe and soft to the touch.**

Planning ahead: Cut the fruit a couple of hours in advance, cover it with cling
film and keep it in the fridge.

Cut all the fruit into small, even cubes then place in a sieve to drain
off the juice. Season the salmon fillets with salt and pepper, turn them in
the oil and cook under a preheated grill for about 3 minutes on each side.
Test with a knife; when cooked, the flesh in the centre should still be
slightly pink and translucent.

While the fish is cooking, gently mix the fruit together, then add the
red onion, tomato, chillies and lime juice. Stir in the mint, then warm the
salsa gently – it should not be hot. Put the fish on heated serving plates
and place a spoonful of the salsa next to it.

STRAWBERRIES IN BALSAMIC VINEGAR

600g (1¼lb) strawberries

100g (3½oz) caster sugar

100ml (3½fl oz) balsamic vinegar

sprig of mint to decorate

peppermill

This is an excellent way of preparing strawberries that are not quite ripe.

Wash, hull and dry the strawberries, then cut them in half
lengthways. Put the sugar and vinegar in a small saucepan and heat until
the sugar is dissolved. Pour over the strawberries and add freshly ground
black pepper. Cover and leave to stand for 1 hour, turning occasionally.
Drain off the vinegar before serving, and decorate with the mint.

AUTUMN MENU ONE

SHALLOT SOUP WITH THYME
ROAST LOIN OF PORK WITH ARTICHOKES
FANTASY OF CHOCOLATE PERFUMED WITH HERBS

SHALLOT SOUP WITH THYME

2 tbsp groundnut oil

750g (1½lb) shallots, peeled and thinly sliced

1 clove of garlic, peeled and crushed

2 medium carrots, peeled and thinly sliced

1 litre (1¾ pints) chicken stock

2 tbsp thyme leaves

3 tbsp double cream

salt and peppermill

Shallots have a more delicate flavour than onions. If you cannot get them, substitute red onions, which are milder and sweeter than normal onions. Do not cut onions a long time before using them, as they develop a bitter flavour. Use only fresh thyme for this soup. You can use lemon thyme but you will need to increase the quantity slightly as it is not quite as strong.

Heat the oil in a heavy-based pan and sweat the shallots without letting them colour for about 5 minutes, until soft. Add the garlic and sweat for a further minute. Add the carrots and chicken stock and simmer, covered, for 5 minutes. Add the thyme and salt and pepper and cook for about 15 minutes, until all the ingredients are tender. Leave to cool, then liquidize until smooth and adjust the seasoning to taste. If necessary, add a little extra stock to thin the soup. Reheat gently and stir in the cream.

ROAST LOIN OF PORK WITH ARTICHOKES

750g (1½lb) eye of loin of pork, with the
rind removed

4 large cloves of garlic (use 8 if garlic is small),
peeled and cut into quarters lengthways

4 tbsp groundnut oil

4 globe artichokes

500g (1lb 1oz) potatoes, peeled, cut into 2cm
(¾ inch) cubes and patted dry

2 sprigs of rosemary

200ml (7fl oz) red wine

75g (2½oz) Home-dried Tomatoes in
Olive Oil (see page 30)

salt and peppermill

After many years of fast breeding and a lot of second-rate meat, a few small producers have returned to more traditional methods to produce very high-quality pork. In the hope that this trend will continue, I have included recipes for pork in this book.

Heat the oven to 220°C/425°F/Gas Mark 7. With a small sharp knife, make deep incisions in the meat and slide a piece of garlic into each. Season generously with salt and pepper.

Heat a roasting tin on the hob, add the oil and the loin of pork and cook until sealed on all sides.

Remove the outside leaves from the artichokes, remove the choke, trim around the base and cut them into quarters. Season the artichokes and potatoes and add them to the roasting tin with the rosemary. Roast in the oven for about 45 minutes until the meat is cooked and the vegetables are lightly coloured and tender. Remove the pork and vegetables from the tin and keep warm.

Add the red wine and the dried tomatoes to the roasting tin, place it on the hob and boil fast until the wine has reduced by a third. Adjust the seasoning. Slice the meat and serve it with the vegetables and sauce.

FANTASY OF CHOCOLATE PERFUMED WITH HERBS

450ml (¾ pint) double cream

2 tbsp fresh lavender flowers

2 tbsp rosemary spikes

2 tbsp thyme leaves

75g (2½oz) plain chocolate, melted

90g (3oz) milk chocolate, melted

100g (3½oz) white chocolate, melted

cocoa powder for dusting

For the orange coulis

juice of 4 oranges

2 tsp cornflour

2 tbsp Grand Marnier

a little sugar (optional)

Planning ahead: Ideally, this needs to be prepared the day before.

Combine 4 tablespoons of the cream with the lavender flowers in a small saucepan and bring to the boil. Leave to infuse for 5 minutes, then pass through a fine sieve. Repeat this procedure with the rosemary and thyme.

Add the lavender cream to the melted plain chocolate, the rosemary cream to the milk chocolate and the thyme cream to the white chocolate. Whip the remaining cream until it forms soft peaks and divide it into 3 equal portions. Fold one into each of the 3 chocolate mixtures. Divide each mixture between 4 tiny ramekin dishes. (In the hotel I use small rings which sit directly on trays. This makes unmoulding so much easier.) Leave to set in the fridge for at least 4 hours, preferably overnight.

For the orange coulis, mix 1 tablespoon of the orange juice with the cornflour. Bring the remaining orange juice to the boil and stir in the cornflour mixture. Cook, stirring, for 1–2 minutes, until lightly thickened. Remove from the heat and stir in the Grand Marnier. If the oranges are very tart, you might like to add a little sugar.

Unmould each ramekin carefully on to a board and neaten the edges as necessary. Dust with cocoa powder. Arrange one of each flavour on each serving plate and pour the orange coulis around.

NOTE: In the picture the Fantasy of Chocolate is served with brandy snap curls. Follow the recipe for brandy snap tulips on page 168 but roll the mixture in thin strips. Once baked (they may need less cooking time), allow to cool for a few seconds, then wrap around a piece of wooden dowelling (or any other tube shape at hand) and leave to set into curls.

TIPS

The herbs must always be fresh and not dried.

You can, of course, simplify this recipe by using only one type of chocolate and one herb.

Fantasy of Chocolate Perfumed with Herbs

AUTUMN MENU TWO

PARFAIT OF PARTRIDGE WITH GRAPES
FILLETS OF HAKE ON MUSHROOM AND SPINACH WITH POTATO RINGS
PLUM AND HAZELNUT TART

PARFAIT OF PARTRIDGE WITH GRAPES

2 partridges (see method)
4 tbsp groundnut oil
½ onion, chopped
½ carrot, chopped
1 celery stick, chopped
4 tbsp brandy
500ml (16fl oz) chicken stock
1 tbsp chopped shallots
300g (10oz) chicken livers, cleaned
300ml (½ pint) double cream
225g (8oz) green grapes, peeled, halved and
pips removed (or use seedless grapes)
salt and peppermill

TIP
It is not worth making this parfait in small amounts and the quantitiy given here will serve 8-12. You could freeze half of it before adding the grapes, or you could serve leftovers on toast as an amuse-gueule at the beginning of a meal.

If you are unlucky enough to buy a pheasant, partridge or grouse that was damaged when it was shot or is badly bruised, make it into a parfait. It is less work than a pâté, the flavour is more refined and the texture smoother.

Ask your butcher to remove the breasts and legs from the partridges, to take off the thigh bone from the legs and to chop the carcass and bones finely. You will then have 4 breasts and the meat from the thighs. Discard the skin.

Heat the oven to maximum temperature. On the hob, heat half the oil in a roasting tin and brown the partridge bones well on all sides, then transfer them to the oven and roast for 15 minutes. Add the vegetables and roast for a further 5 minutes. Remove from the oven and pour away the fat. Place the roasting tin on the hob, add three-quarters of the brandy and ignite, standing well back. When the flames have died down, add the chicken stock and then boil fast to reduce by two-thirds, stirring occasionally and skimming frequently.

Reduce the oven temperature to 190°C/375°F/Gas Mark 5. Trim all the meat from the partridge breasts and thighs and cut it into small cubes. Heat 1 tablespoon of the remaining oil in a small pan and sweat the shallots until translucent. In an ovenproof casserole, heat the remaining oil and cook the partridge meat quickly over a high heat until sealed on all sides. Add the chicken livers and cooked shallots, season, then cover and place in the oven for about 10 minutes, until the livers are cooked but still pink. Remove from the oven and add the reduced stock.

Leave to cool and then pass the mixture through a very fine mincer plate or purée it in a food processor. Whip the cream and gently fold it into the meat, then add the remaining brandy and season with salt and pepper. Chill for several hours, then garnish with the grapes just before serving. Serve with warm French bread or toasted brioche.

FILLETS OF HAKE ON MUSHROOM AND SPINACH WITH POTATO RINGS

2 medium potatoes (about 400g/14oz)

80g (2½oz) unsalted clarified butter

4 x 150g (5oz) hake fillets, all bones removed, skin left on

2 tbsp groundnut oil

30g (1oz) onion, finely chopped

2 cloves of garlic, peeled and crushed

100g (3½oz) mushrooms, sliced

400g (14oz) spinach, blanched and squeezed dry

4 tbsp double cream

salt and peppermill

Hake has a firmer flesh than cod and fries or grills very well.

Planning ahead: The potato rings can be made a day in advance and reheated. They may also be used for many other dishes or as a garnish.

Peel the potatoes and cut them in very thin slices – less than 3mm (⅛ inch) thick. Using a 3cm (1¼ inch) round metal cutter, cut out a batch of slices at a time to give you perfectly shaped rounds. Cut a 2cm (¾ inch) hole in the centre of each one with a cutter.

Heat 60g (2oz) of the butter in a large non-stick frying pan and arrange a quarter of the potato rings overlapping in a round shape, about 10cm (4 inch) in diameter. Repeat with the remaining slices to make 3 more rings. Ensure the potatoes are just covered in the butter. Cook the potato rings over a gentle heat for about 3 minutes until golden brown. The potatoes should be crisp and sticking together.

Preheat the oven to 200°C/400°F/Gas Mark 6. Season the hake with salt and pepper. Heat the oil in a frying pan and cook the fish over a high heat for about 1 minute on each side, until the skin is very crispy. Transfer to a shallow tin or baking tray and cook in the oven for 3–5 minutes, depending on thickness. Test the fish with the point of a knife; the flesh in the centre should be translucent.

Heat the remaining butter in a saucepan, add the onion and sweat until soft. Add the garlic and sweat for a further minute. Add the mushrooms and cook quickly over a high heat until the liquid has evaporated. Add the spinach and season with salt and pepper. In a small saucepan, boil the cream until reduced by half, the add it to the spinach mixture. Adjust the seasoning, spoon the spinach mixture on to serving plates, then top with the hake and arrange the potato rings on top.

PLUM AND HAZELNUT TART

200g (7oz) puff pastry

Frangipane (see page 70)

30g (1oz) hazelnuts, finely chopped

12 red plums, stoned and thinly sliced

20g (¾oz) unsalted butter

45g (1½oz) caster sugar

Planning ahead: This can be made 6 hours in advance, then warmed to serve.

Heat the oven to 220°C/425°F/Gas Mark 7. On a lightly floured surface, roll out the pastry until it is 3mm (⅛ inch) thick and cut out a 25cm (10 inch) round. Place on a buttered baking sheet, prick all over with a fork and leave to rest in the fridge for about 20 minutes.

Spread the frangipane evenly over the puff pastry, then sprinkle on the hazelnuts. Arrange the sliced plums on top. Melt the butter with the sugar and brush on to the plums.

Bake the tart in the oven for 25 minutes, then place a piece of baking parchment and a second baking sheet on top of the tart and turn it upside down. Bake upside down for 15 minutes to ensure that the pastry is crisp. Leave to cool, then turn the right way up and remove the paper.

AUTUMN MENU THREE

MUSHROOM SALAD
RABBIT WITH GINGER, MUSTARD AND POLENTA
BLUEBERRY GRATIN

MUSHROOM SALAD

8 shallots, unpeeled

4 tbsp olive oil

1 large fennel bulb (at least 225g/8oz),
trimmed and cut into 6mm (¼ inch) dice

1 large carrot, peeled and cut into 6mm
(¼ inch) dice

180g (6oz) mixed wild mushrooms, sliced
if large

1 tbsp chopped chives

8 basil leaves, cut into thin strips

2 tbsp balsamic vinegar

salt and peppermill

Wild mushrooms without doubt are a great delicacy. The foremost varieties are cèpes, chanterelles, black trumpets and oyster mushrooms – there are many others of course. The experts' opinions differ when it comes to the preparation of wild mushrooms. Some just clean and wash them quickly (in the case of cèpes many do not wash these) and then cook them together with shallots and a little garlic, herbs and seasoning. Others blanch them very quickly. My advice is when using small quantities, just quickly fry in butter with shallots and garlic. When using larger quantities, blanch them first and then proceed as mentioned above.

Preheat the oven to 200°C/400°F/Gas Mark 6. Place the shallots on a piece of aluminium foil and drizzle with a little of the olive oil. Wrap and bake for about 30 minutes, until tender.

Blanch the fennel and carrot separately, then drain and refresh in iced water. Dry on a kitchen cloth. Heat half the remaining oil in a heavy-based pan, add the fennel and cook for about 5 minutes, until almost soft. Add the carrot and continue cooking for another few minutes until soft. Season with salt and pepper. In a separate pan, heat the remaining oil, add the wild mushrooms and toss until heated through. Season with salt and pepper and stir in the chives.

Spoon the fennel mixture into the centre of each serving plate and level the surface. Top with the mushroom mixture. Cut the shallots in half lengthways and arrange 4 pieces around each plate. Sprinkle the basil over the plates and drizzle with the balsamic vinegar. Serve lukewarm.

MUSHROOM SALAD, RABBIT WITH GINGER, MUSTARD AND POLENTA, AND BLUEBERRY GRATIN

RABBIT WITH GINGER, MUSTARD AND POLENTA

1 rabbit (see method)

4 tbsp grain mustard

2 tbsp plain flour

2 tbsp groundnut oil

100g (3½oz) unsalted butter

1 onion, peeled and finely chopped

1 clove of garlic, peeled and crushed

1 tsp freshly grated ginger

2 tbsp tarragon vinegar

2 tbsp medium sweet sherry

1.2 litres (2 pints) chicken stock

180g (6oz) instant polenta

4 plum tomatoes, blanched, peeled, deseeded and diced

2 tbsp chopped tarragon

75g (2½oz) Parmesan cheese, freshly grated

100ml (3½fl oz) double cream

tarragon leaves

salt and peppermill

Serve this dish with a rocket and spinach salad.

Planning ahead: The rabbit can be cooked 3 hours in advance. Do not overcook the meat or it will obviously dry up when you reheat it.

Ask your butcher to joint the rabbit so that you have 10 pieces: the legs cut in half, the saddle cut in 4 pieces and the shoulders.

Preheat the oven to 200°C/400°F/Gas Mark 6. Season the meat with salt and pepper, then brush the mustard on generously and dust with the flour. Heat half the oil in a heavy-based ovenproof pan or a roasting tin, then add the rabbit pieces and 20g (¾oz) of the butter. Keep turning the pieces until they have a good colour, then transfer to the oven and cook for 15 minutes until the meat is tender. Remove the rabbit pieces from the pan and pour away the fat.

To make the sauce, add the remaining oil and 30g (1oz) of the remaining butter to the pan in which the rabbit was cooked. Add the onion and sweat until soft. Add the garlic and ginger and sweat for a further minute. Stir in the vinegar and sherry and boil fast until reduced by half. Add 400ml (14fl oz) of the chicken stock and cook until reduced by two-thirds.

Meanwhile, in a separate pan bring the remaining chicken stock to the boil. Add the rest of the butter and the polenta and stir vigorously, then reduce the heat, cover and cook very gently for 5–10 minutes, stirring frequently.

Return the rabbit pieces to the sauce and heat through gently. Stir in the tomatoes and tarragon and adjust the seasoning. Stir the Parmesan cheese and cream into the polenta and season with salt and pepper. Serve the rabbit accompanied by the polenta, and garnished with the tarragon.

TIPS

This recipe also works well with chicken pieces.

Instead of polenta you can serve fresh pasta.

BLUEBERRY GRATIN

3 egg yolks
45g (1½oz) caster sugar
45g (1½oz) eau de vie de framboise
4 tbsp double cream, semi-whipped
300g (10oz) blueberries

An incredibly quick dessert which has a maximum impact! You can use other fruit, such as mango, pawpaw, strawberries or raspberries.

Put the egg yolks and sugar in a bowl with the eau de vie. Place the bowl over a pan of simmering water and whisk continously until the mixture has trebled in volume, to make a sabayon. Remove from the heat and continue whisking until the sabayon is cold. Fold in the cream.

Divide the blueberries between 4 individual gratin dishes and cover with the sabayon. Place under a preheated grill for 3–4 minutes until glazed to a golden brown colour.

WINTER MENU ONE

SALAD OF CRAB WITH AVOCADO
LAMB FILLETS ON AUBERGINE PURÉE WITH MEDITERRANEAN SALSA
PECAN AND CHOCOLATE DELIGHT

SALAD OF CRAB WITH AVOCADO

200g (7oz) white crab meat

3 tbsp mayonnaise

a drop of Tabasco sauce

a few drops of Worcestershire sauce

2 tbsp sherry vinegar

6 tbsp extra virgin olive oil

2 avocados, peeled, stoned and finely cubed

4 plum tomatoes, blanched, peeled, deseeded and finely diced

60g (2oz) curly endive, the yellow heart only

4 sprigs of dill

10g (¼oz) chives, cut into 3cm (1¼ inch) lengths

salt and peppermill

The best crab to use is the large queen crab. However, you will then have to find some use for the brown meat. Alternatively, you can buy vacuum-packed white crab meat.
Instead of white crab meat, you could use prawns or small pieces of poached fish.

Check the crab meat carefully to make sure it doesn't contain any shell, then mix it with the mayonnaise, Tabasco, Worcestershire sauce and seasoning.

Mix the sherry vinegar with the oil to make a dressing and season with salt and pepper. Mix the avocado with three-quarters of the tomato, season with salt and pepper and add half the dressing.

Place a 10cm (4 inch) cutter in the centre of a serving plate, half fill with the avocado mixture and then top this with the same amount of the crab mixture. Remove the cutter and repeat on 3 more serving plates.

Toss the remaining tomatoes in a little of the remaining dressing and adjust the seasoning. Spoon on top of the crab meat and garnish with the sprigs of dill.

Toss the curly endive with the remaining dressing, adjust the seasoning and arrange on the plates around the crab. Garnish the curly endive with the chives.

TIP
The dispelling of the avocado myth: to prevent them discolouring, place the avocado cubes in a non-stick pan and heat slightly under the grill, tossing a few times. The avocado will now retain its colour for 2-3 hours.

LAMB FILLETS ON AUBERGINE PURÉE WITH MEDITERRANEAN SALSA

1 small onion, peeled and finely chopped

2 tbsp groundnut oil

450g (1lb) aubergine, peeled and cubed

4 baby aubergines

a little olive oil

4 cherry tomatoes

1 tbsp freshly grated Parmesan cheese

2 lamb fillets from the eye of the loin

salt and peppermill

For the salsa

1 red pepper

1 large Baked Onion in Balsamic Vinegar (see
page 31)

6 Pan-fried Garlic Cloves (see page 23)

15g (½oz) pitted black olives

15g (½oz) pitted green olives

20g (¾oz) pine kernels, toasted

8 tbsp extra virgin olive oil

½ tsp finely chopped chilli

1 tbsp chopped basil

Salsas are a recent import from Mexico, Spain and, of course, America. They have many advantages for the home cook, since they are healthier and easier to prepare than more time-consuming sauces.

To make the aubergine purée, sweat the onion in half the groundnut oil until translucent. Add the cubed aubergine, cover and cook over a gentle heat without colouring until very soft, stirring frequently. Season with salt and pepper. Cool slightly, then purée in a food processor and adjust the seasoning.

Rub the baby aubergines with a little olive oil and place under a preheated grill for 5 minutes just until the skin softens, turning once or twice. Peel the aubergines and cut each one almost through into 4 slices, leaving them attached at the stalk end. Cut each cherry tomato into 3 slices and tuck them between the slices of aubergine. Season with salt and pepper. Place on a buttered baking tray and sprinkle with the Parmesan cheese, then set aside.

For the salsa, grill the red pepper until charred and blistered on all sides. Place in a paper bag for 5 minutes or until cool enough to handle, then peel, removing the core and membranes. Cut the pepper, balsamic onion, pan-fried garlic and black and green olives into fine strips. Toss with the pine kernels, olive oil and chilli and season with salt and pepper.

Preheat the oven to 200°C/400°F/Gas Mark 6. Cut each fillet of lamb in half crossways and season with salt and pepper. Heat the remaining groundnut oil in a roasting tin on the hob, add the meat and cook until sealed on all sides. Put the baby aubergines in the oven until heated through. Roast the lamb for about 4 minutes, until pink in the centre, then leave to rest in a warm place.

Reheat the aubergine purée. Put the salsa in a pan and heat gently, then stir in the basil. Place some of the hot aubergine purée on each plate. Slice the fillet of lamb lengthways and arrange on top of the aubergine purée. Garnish with the baby aubergine and serve with the salsa.

LAMB FILLETS ON AUBERGINE PURÉE WITH MEDITERRANEAN SALSA

PECAN AND CHOCOLATE DELIGHT

200g (7oz) pecan nuts

75g (2½oz) caster sugar

60g (2oz) unsalted butter

150ml (¼ pint) double cream

180g (6oz) good-quality plain chocolate, chopped

2 tbsp Grand Marnier

Prepare this dessert a day in advance.

Preheat the oven to 200°C/400°F/Gas Mark 6. Put the pecans and sugar in a food processor and work until smooth. Melt half the butter, pour it on to the nut mixture and process until well mixed. Place the pecan mixture in a 20cm (8 inch) flan tin and press it firmly over the base and sides to form a crust. Bake blind for 20 minutes, until lightly coloured, then leave to cool.

Bring the cream to the boil in a saucepan and remove from the heat. Dice the remaining butter and whisk it into the cream with the chocolate until all the chocolate has melted. Stir in the Grand Marnier. Pour the chocolate filling into the pecan crust and refrigerate overnight.

WINTER MENU TWO

Potato Gnocchi on Duck Ragout
Fillets of Pork in Thai Curry Sauce with Fragrant Rice
Key Lime Pie

POTATO GNOCCHI ON DUCK RAGOUT

2 tbsp groundnut oil

1 onion, peeled and finely chopped

3 cloves of garlic, peeled and crushed

1 carrot, peeled and finely chopped

1 celery stick, peeled and finely chopped

1 small leek, trimmed and chopped

4 duck legs off the bone, all skin removed and meat minced

2 tbsp tomato purée

300ml (½ pint) red wine

600ml (1 pint) chicken stock

½ bay leaf

1 sprig of rosemary

45g (1½oz) Parmesan cheese, freshly grated

30g (1oz) unsalted butter

8 sage leaves

salt and peppermill

For the gnocchi

400g (14oz) floury potatoes

100g (3½oz) plain flour

½ egg, beaten

pinch of freshly grated nutmeg

TIP
Make sure the potatoes are hot when mixed with the other ingredients.

Good gnocchi are the pride and joy of every Italian housewife. You may need a little practice to get really good results but providing you use floury potatoes such as King Edward or Pentland Crown you should not have a problem.

Planning ahead: The ragout can be made a few days in advance. It also freezes well although you should add some more herbs when reheating.

Heat the oil in a large saucepan and sweat the onion until translucent, then add the garlic and sweat for a further minute. Add the carrot, celery and leek and cook until slightly coloured. Add the minced duck and cook over a high heat until well browned, then stir in the tomato purée and cook for 2–3 minutes. Add the red wine and boil fast until reduced by three-quarters. Add the chicken stock and herbs and simmer, uncovered, for 30 minutes. Adjust the seasoning.

To make the gnocchi, cook the potatoes in their skins in boiling salted water until tender. Drain and cool slightly, then peel and return to the pan. Dry them out over a low heat, then mash them thoroughly and mix in the flour and egg. Season with salt, pepper and nutmeg. Shape the mixture into about 40 small balls and press them lightly with a fork to give a ridged surface. Bring a large pan of salted water to the boil, drop in the gnocchi and cook just until they rise to the surface, about 1–2 minutes. (Don't crowd the pan; cook the gnocchi in batches if necessary.) Remove from the pan with a slotted spoon and drain thoroughly.

Spoon the duck sauce on to deep heatproof serving plates and arrange the gnocchi on top. Sprinkle with the Parmesan cheese and place under a preheated grill until lightly coloured. Heat the butter in a small pan. When it froths and turns slightly brown, add the sage leaves and cook for 2–3 seconds. Then arrange the leaves on top of the gnocchi and pour over the butter.

FILLETS OF PORK IN THAI CURRY SAUCE WITH FRAGRANT RICE

30g (1oz) onion, peeled and chopped

4 tbsp vegetable oil

180g (6oz) Thai fragrant rice

750ml (1¼ pints) chicken stock, warmed

pinch of saffron

45g (1½oz) butter

20g (¾oz) flaked almonds, toasted

8 x 50g (1¾oz) pieces of pork fillet (tenderloin)

1 tbsp finely chopped fresh ginger

2 cloves of garlic, peeled and crushed

¼ tsp green peppercorns

1 lemon grass stalk, finely chopped

2 tsp chopped fresh chilli

1 tsp lime juice

½ tsp ground coriander

400ml (14fl oz) coconut milk

½ green pepper, peeled and finely diced

½ red pepper, peeled and finely diced

2 tsp chopped coriander

salt and peppermill

Sweat the onion in half the oil until translucent, then add the rice and stir to coat with the oil. Add 600ml (1 pint) hot chicken stock and the saffron. Season, then cover and cook gently until the rice is tender and all the stock has been absorbed. Mix in 15g (½oz) butter and the almonds.

Season the pork fillets with salt and pepper. Fry in 15g (½oz) of the butter and the remaining oil until well browned on all sides and just cooked in the centre, about 5 minutes. Remove from the pan and keep them warm.

For the sauce, melt half the remaining butter in a pan and sauté the ginger, garlic, peppercorns, lemon grass and chilli for 1–2 minutes. Add the remaining chicken stock, plus the lime juice and ground coriander. Gradually stir in the coconut milk, then bring to the boil, reduce the heat and simmer, uncovered, for about 10 minutes. Cool slightly, then purée in a liquidizer and pass through a fine sieve.

Heat the remaining butter in a pan and toss the diced peppers in it. Reheat the sauce gently, stir in the chopped coriander and season to taste.

Divide the rice between 4 serving plates and arrange the pork fillets on top. Sprinkle with the peppers and pour the sauce over.

KEY LIME PIE

250g (8½oz) Sweet Pastry (see page 37)

4 egg yolks

165g (5½oz) caster sugar

2 tsp finely grated lime zest

100ml (3½fl oz) lime juice (about 4 limes)

2 egg whites

lightly whipped cream and strawberries to decorate (optional)

On a lightly floured work surface, roll out the pastry to 3mm (⅛ inch) thick and use to line a deep 20cm (8 inch) flan tin. Chill for at least 20 minutes. Preheat the oven to 190°C/375°F/Gas Mark 5. Bake the pastry blind for 15 minutes, then remove the baking beans and bake for a further 10–15 minutes, until golden brown. Reduce the oven temperature to 180°C/350°F/Gas Mark 4.

Put the egg yolks in a bowl set over a pan of hot water and whisk until light and fluffy and doubled in volume. Whisk in 100g (3½oz) of the sugar, then remove the bowl from the pan and whisk in the lime zest and lime juice.

Heat the remaining sugar on a piece of greaseproof paper in the oven for a few minutes. Whisk the egg whites in a bowl until they form soft peaks, then add the warm sugar a spoonful at a time, whisking to a medium-firm peak. Fold the egg whites into the lime mixture. Transfer to the pastry case and bake for about 20 minutes, until lightly set. Cool and then refrigerate. Decorate with whipped cream and strawberries before serving, if wished.

TIP

Traditionally, key limes are used in this American dessert but these are hard to obtain in the UK. You could use half lime juice and half lemon juice to give a flavour closer to that of key limes.

WINTER MENU THREE

POACHED EGG ON ARTICHOKE BOTTOMS WITH PISTACHIO MAYONNAISE
LENTIL AND POLENTA CAKES WITH CUCUMBER AND YOGHURT SAUCE
PEARS WITH BUTTERSCOTCH SAUCE

POACHED EGG ON ARTICHOKE BOTTOMS WITH PISTACHIO MAYONNAISE

4 globe artichokes

1 lemon, cut in half

30g (1oz) plain flour

100ml (3½fl oz) white wine vinegar

4 eggs

1 tbsp sherry vinegar

3 tbsp extra virgin olive oil

4 small handfuls of curly endive, sliced
radicchio and corn salad

salt and peppermill

For the mayonnaise

200ml (7fl oz) mayonnaise

2 tbsp chopped coriander

4 tbsp pistachio nuts, blanched in milk,
skinned and finely chopped

2 tbsp tomato ketchup

Tabasco sauce

a little vegetable or chicken stock

TIP

When poaching eggs, never add salt to
the water because it prevents the white
closing properly around the yolks.

Planning ahead: The poached egg can be prepared a day in advance and kept in cold water in the fridge. Reheat briefly in salted water.

Break the stalks from the artichokes, pull off the large side leaves and then cut off all the smaller leaves at the top. When you reach the hairy choke, scoop it out. Trim any remaining leaves or stalk from the artichoke bottoms and rub all over with a lemon half to prevent discoloration.

Bring about 1 litre (1¾ pints) of water to the boil, then add salt and the other lemon half. Mix the flour with a little cold water and stir into the boiling water. Put the artichokes in the pan and simmer for approximately 10–15 minutes, until tender but still firm. Drain, refresh in iced water and drain again.

Bring 1 litre (1¾ pints) of water and the white wine vinegar to the boil in a small, deep pan and reduce the heat to simmering point. Crack each egg into a cup, then slide it gently into the simmering water. Simmer for about 3 minutes or until all the egg white has closed around the yolk. Lift the eggs out of the pan and slide them into a bowl of cold water. This stops the cooking and will also wash off the taste of the vinegar. Drain on a clean tea towel and trim off any straggly bits. Cover and keep to one side.

Mix the mayonnaise with the pistachios, coriander, tomato ketchup and a few drops of Tabasco, adding a little vegetable or chicken stock as necessary to make a smooth coating consistency. Warm the artichoke bottoms and poached eggs in a little salted water for about 1½ minutes and dry on a tea towel.

Mix the sherry vinegar with the olive oil to make a dressing and season with salt and pepper. Toss the salad leaves with the dressing and adjust the seasoning. Arrange the salad on serving plates, set an artichoke bottom in the centre of each one and top with an egg. Cover the eggs with the pistachio mayonnaise.

LENTIL AND POLENTA CAKES WITH CUCUMBER AND YOGHURT SAUCE

300g (10oz) Puy lentils

200ml (7fl oz) vegetable stock

90g (3oz) fine polenta

30g (1oz) Parmesan cheese, freshly grated

1 egg, beaten

1 tsp dried chilli flakes

75g (2½oz) leek, finely chopped and
blanched

1 tbsp balsamic vinegar

5 tbsp olive oil

225g (8oz) small new potatoes in their skins,
cut into quarters

2 tbsp Home-dried Tomatoes in Olive Oil (see
page 30)

2 tbsp chopped chives (optional)

salt and peppermill

For the sauce

½ cucumber, thinly sliced

200ml (7fl oz) natural yoghurt

1 clove of garlic, crushed

Planning ahead: The polenta cakes can be made up to 12 hours before frying. The cucumber and yoghurt sauce will keep for 2 days covered in the fridge.

Wash the lentils and cook in plenty of salted water for about 25 minutes, until tender but still firm. Drain, refresh in iced water and dry well on a clean tea towel.

Bring the vegetable stock to the boil, add a pinch of salt and stir in the polenta. Cook gently, stirring, until thickened. Stir in the Parmesan cheese and egg and adjust the seasoning. Mix together the lentils, polenta, chilli flakes and leek. Adjust the seasoning, cool then shape into 4 round cakes. Leave in the fridge for at least 1 hour or overnight until firm.

Preheat the oven to 180°C/350°F/Gas Mark 4. Mix the balsamic vinegar with 3 tablespoons of the olive oil to make a dressing and season with salt and pepper. Toss the potato quarters in the dressing, then arrange them on a baking tray and bake for about 45 minutes, until tender, turning occasionally. Heat the dried tomatoes in the oven with the potatoes for the last few minutes of the cooking time.

For the sauce, put the cucumber slices in boiling salted water for 2 seconds, then drain, refresh in iced water and dry. Mix with the yoghurt and garlic.

Heat the remaining oil in a non-stick frying pan and cook the polenta cakes for about 3–4 minutes on each side, until heated through and well browned. Spoon some cucumber and yoghurt sauce on to each serving plate and place a polenta cake in the middle. Top with a little more sauce, then garnish with the potatoes and tomatoes and sprinkle with the chopped chives, if using.

POACHED EGG ON ARTICHOKE BOTTOMS WITH PISTACHIO MAYONNAISE, LENTIL AND POLENTA CAKES WITH
CUCUMBER AND YOGHURT SAUCE, AND PEARS WITH BUTTERSCOTCH SAUCE

Pears with Butterscotch Sauce

45g (1½oz) maple syrup

45g (1½oz) golden syrup

45g (1½oz) soft brown sugar

120ml (4fl oz) double cream

60g (2oz) unsalted butter

4 ripe pears

juice of 1 lemon

30g (1oz) caster sugar

vanilla ice cream to serve

sprigs of mint to decorate

Planning ahead: Make the butterscotch sauce 2-3 hours in advance.

To make the butterscotch sauce, put the maple syrup, golden syrup and brown sugar in a pan and bring to the boil. Add the cream and half the butter and bring back to the boil, then remove from the heat.

Peel the pears and cut each one into 6 wedges, removing the cores, then toss in the lemon juice. Melt the remaining butter in a frying pan, add the pears and sprinkle over the caster sugar. Cook over a moderate heat until the pears are soft and caramelized. Transfer to warmed serving plates and pour the sauce over the pears. Serve with vanilla ice cream and decorate with sprigs of mint.

TIP

Press the pears gently when you buy them: they should be ripe yet firm, so they do not become mushy when cooked. Best varieties are Comice and Packham.

WINTER MENU FOUR

WARM RABBIT ON TOMATO AND APPLE CHUTNEY WITH BABY SPINACH
SEA BREAM WITH CRAB AND HERB CRUST AND SPICY VEGETABLE SAUCE
BRANDY SNAP WITH EXOTIC FRUIT AND GINGER ICE CREAM

WARM RABBIT ON TOMATO AND APPLE CHUTNEY WITH BABY SPINACH

1 saddle of rabbit

2 tbsp groundnut oil

1–2 tbsp balsamic vinegar

2 tbsp extra virgin olive oil

1 tsp Dijon mustard

1 tbsp double cream

4 large handfuls of baby spinach

20g (¾oz) Parmesan cheese, cut into shavings

salt and peppermill

For the chutney

½ onion, peeled and finely chopped

4 tomatoes, cut into 1cm (⅓ inch) cubes

2 dessert apples, peeled, cored and cut into

1cm (⅓ inch) cubes

½ tsp mixed spice

½ tsp freshly grated ginger

100ml (3½fl oz) white wine vinegar

juice of ½ lemon

75g (2½oz) caster sugar

The tomato and apple chutney also goes well with poultry.

Planning ahead: Prepare the chutney in advance. It will keep for a few weeks in the fridge.

To make the chutney, place all the ingredients in a heavy-based pan, cover and simmer for 30 minutes, stirring occasionally. Remove the lid and continue cooking for a further 15 minutes.

Preheat the oven to 220°C/425°F/Gas Mark 7. Season the saddle of rabbit. Heat the groundnut oil in a roasting tin on the hob and brown the rabbit well on all sides, then transfer to the oven and roast for 15 minutes. To test the meat, press with a fingertip; if it is slightly springy it should be done. Rest the rabbit in a warm place for 10 minutes, then take the fillets off the bone. Don't forget the 2 fillets under the bone.

Mix together the balsamic vinegar, olive oil, mustard and cream to make a dressing and season with salt and pepper. Place a generous spoonful of the warm chutney on each plate. Cut the rabbit fillets in thin slices at an angle and arrange in a circle on top of the chutney. Toss the spinach with the dressing and adjust the seasoning. Arrange around the meat and sprinkle the Parmesan cheese shavings on top of the spinach.

SEA BREAM WITH CRAB AND HERB CRUST AND SPICY VEGETABLE SAUCE

30g (1oz) unsalted butter

1 tsp freshly grated ginger

120g (4oz) white crab meat

1 tbsp finely chopped parsley

1 tbsp finely chopped basil

4 x 120g (4oz) sea bream fillets, all bones removed, skin left on

1 tbsp vegetable oil

15g (½oz) Parmesan cheese, freshly grated

salt and peppermill

Spicy Vegetable Sauce (see below)

Heat the butter and ginger in a small pan and cook gently for 1 minute. Remove from the heat and stir in the crab meat, herbs and salt and pepper to taste. Season the fish and fry quickly in the vegetable oil in a non-stick pan for 1 minute on each side; the skin side should be crispy but do not overcook. Spread the crab mixture on top and sprinkle lightly with the grated Parmesan. Place under a preheated grill until the crust is lightly coloured and the fish is cooked through. Serve with the sauce.

SPICY VEGETABLE SAUCE

Makes 450ml (¾ pint)

30g (1oz) unsalted butter

1½ tbsp vegetable oil

1 onion, peeled and finely chopped

1 red pepper, deseeded and finely chopped

1 small dessert apple, peeled, cored and chopped

½ tsp curry powder

pinch of saffron

350ml (12fl oz) chicken stock

3 tbsp double cream or crème fraîche

salt and peppermill

This versatile sauce goes well with fish, poultry and pasta and is ideal with vegetable dishes.

Planning ahead: This can be prepared in advance; just reheat and add the cream at the last moment.

Heat the butter and oil in a saucepan and cook the onion gently until soft and translucent, stirring frequently. Stir in the red pepper, then cover and cook gently for 10 minutes. Add the apple to the pan with the curry powder and saffron, stir well, then cook, covered, for a further 5 minutes. Add 300ml (½ pint) of the chicken stock and bring to the boil. Simmer, covered, for 20 minutes, then leave to cool.

Purée the sauce in a blender or food processor, then stir in the remaining stock and season with salt and pepper. Reheat and stir in the cream before serving.

TIP

To achieve a very smooth consistency, pass the puréed sauce through a fine sieve.

BRANDY SNAP WITH EXOTIC FRUIT AND GINGER ICE CREAM

½ pawpaw

½ mango

½ small melon

1 kiwi fruit

½ small pineapple

Mango Coulis (see below)

sprigs of mint to decorate

For the brandy snap tulips

30g (1oz) unsalted butter

30g (1oz) plain flour

60g (2oz) caster sugar

2 tbsp golden syrup

For the ice cream

250ml (8fl oz) milk

250ml (8fl oz) double cream

100g (3½oz) caster sugar

6 egg yolks

60g (2oz) preserved stem ginger, finely chopped

Planning ahead: The ice cream, brandy snap tulips and mango coulis can be made a day in advance. Store the brandy snaps in an airtight plastic container.

First make the brandy snap tulips. Preheat the oven to 200°C/400°F/Gas Mark 6. Mix the butter, flour and sugar together until the texture resembles breadcrumbs. Add the golden syrup and mix to a paste. Divide into 4 balls and press them out thinly on buttered baking trays, 2 to a tray as they will spread in the oven. Bake them 2 at a time for about 7 minutes, until golden brown. Allow to cool for a few seconds, then mould each one over an inverted ramekin dish to form a tulip shape and leave to set hard. If the brandy snaps harden before you have the chance to shape them, return them to the oven for a few seconds to soften.

For the ice cream, put the milk, cream and sugar in a pan and bring to the boil. Beat the yolks until pale, then pour on the cream mixture, stirring constantly. Return to the pan and stir over a gentle heat until the mixture thickens slightly and coats the back of a wooden spoon. Do not let it boil or it will curdle. Pass through a fine sieve and cool, then stir in the ginger. Freeze in an ice-cream machine according to the manufacturer's instructions. Alternatively, pour into a large freezerproof bowl, cover and freeze until almost set. Transfer to a food processor and whisk until it is creamy and all the ice crystals have broken down. Put the mixture back in the bowl, cover and refreeze. Repeat this process twice, then freeze until firm.

To serve, peel and prepare the fruit, and cut into even-sized pieces. Pour a little mango coulis on each plate and set a brandy snap tulip in the centre. Half fill with fruit, top with a scoop of ice cream and decorate with the mint.

MANGO COULIS

Makes 450ml (¾ pint)

150ml (¼ pint) water

60g (2oz) caster sugar

1 large ripe mango, peeled, stoned and chopped

1 tsp lemon juice

Put the water and sugar in a pan and heat gently until the sugar is dissolved, then leave to cool. Using a hand blender or liquidizer, whizz the mango with the lemon juice and sugar syrup, then pass through a fine sieve.

BRANDY SNAP WITH EXOTIC FRUIT AND GINGER ICE CREAM

KITCHEN TALK

HERBS

Use herbs and bring sunshine to your food! Just as the sun gives colour, depth and definition to a landscape so herbs bring flavour and colour to a dish.

The marriage between certain herbs and foods is long established. Dill with salmon or cucumber salad, tarragon with chicken and fish, rosemary with roast lamb, sage with veal and poultry are all highly successful partnerships. Oregano, a relative of the milder marjoram, goes well with pasta and, like basil, it is an excellent partner for tomatoes. In a similar way, some herbs are closely linked with certain countries. The name oregano comes from the Greek word meaning 'joy of the mountains' and it is an essential part of Greek cuisine. We associate caraway seeds with Germany and Austria, mint with England, thyme with France, and borage with North Africa and the Middle East.

Mint is a champion among herbs. It goes well with fruit in desserts, matches new potatoes perfectly and brings summer-garden aroma to salads. 'Traditional' mint sauce, by which I mean dull green leaves floating in a pool of malt vinegar, is a disaster. Far better to serve your lamb with a mint and apple jelly.

The darlings of *nouvelle cuisine* used to be chives, basil, coriander and tarragon. Arguably they became overused for a time but do not let that put you off! These sensational herbs can transform simple salads, sauces and fish dishes into memorable meals. Remember, too, that the list of herbs is endless. There are many others that are just as versatile and rich in flavour – bergamot, lemon balm, fennel, thyme, watercress, rosemary, sorrel, sage, bay, parsley and the elegant and pretty chervil.

Fresh herbs are always best. If you can't find fresh ones, however, you can in some cases substitute good-quality dried herbs. Use them sparingly and remember that it takes about two or three minutes for their flavour to develop.

Always chop herbs at the last possible moment so they retain their natural oils, which carry the flavour and aroma. Add them to the dish just before serving, otherwise they become tasteless and discoloured.

Best of all, grow your own herbs. They make beautiful plants and many have attractive flowers which you can add to salads. A herb garden can be a large, formal *potager* or simply a few terracotta pots on a patio or windowsill. Both can give enormous pleasure.

If, in the summer months, you have more fresh herbs than you can use, why not dry them yourself? Nothing could be easier! Pick them early in the morning after the dew has dried but before the heat of the day. Remove the stalks and spread the herbs in a single layer on a piece of muslin stretched across a frame, then leave them for about a week in a dry, dark room. When they are ready, store them in an airtight tin or jar.

SEASONING

Show me the person who adds salt and pepper *before* tasting their food and I will show you a philistine. If after tasting, seasoning is needed to counteract the blandness of the food, the finger of blame passes from the diner to the cook.

Food must be seasoned correctly. That is something every cook has to understand. The right balance of seasoning brings out the flavours of the food and helps preserve the colour and texture. That perfect balance will, of course, be different for every dish. In some, the flavour-carrying properties of onions and garlic play their part, while in others you will need to balance salt and pepper with herbs and spices.

I follow a simple rule for salt and pepper – you cannot add later what you do not add at the beginning. The one exception is offal such as liver and kidneys, which should be seasoned as they come out of the pan or off the grill. (If you are preparing a stew, however, with kidneys, for example, you do need to season them in advance.) Adding seasoning at the start achieves a better flavour and means you need to use less. Another way of reducing your salt intake is to use herbs and spices. They are not a complete replacement for seasoning but because they enhance the flavour of food, less salt is needed.

Cold food always requires more seasoning than hot. If you prepare a cold soup, such as the Clear Chilled Tomato Soup on page 76, you will need to overcompensate with the seasoning so that when the soup cools down and loses flavour the balance will be right. By quickly cooling down just a spoonful of the hot soup, you can check whether the seasoning is correct. If the recipe calls for ingredients to be poached in stock it is important to heat the stock *before* you add the seasoning.

Even when you blanch vegetables or boil potatoes, always make sure the water is well seasoned. Taste the water with a spoon as though it were a broth or a sauce.

Taste and taste again! Take care with seasoning and your food will have a wonderful depth and intensity of flavour.

ONIONS AND GARLIC

If nature had not provided us with onions and garlic, cooks would have had to invent them. They are the uncrowned kings of the kitchen. Nothing carries flavour like the humble onion and the often neglected garlic. Without them we could not achieve the blending, infusing and depth of flavour that we take for granted.

There are many varieties of onion but they can be divided here into four main categories: red, green and spring onions and the finely textured shallot. In my kitchen I use shallots for their elegance of flavour. If you cannot obtain them, use green or spring onions. I rarely eat spring onions raw, since I find that their taste is so strong it kills the palate and dominates any other flavours. If the dish you are cooking calls for marinated or raw onions, always use the sweeter red varieties.

A lot of people shy away from using onions. That is a great pity because the consequences they fear – an unpleasant smell on the breath and an unwelcome habit of 'repeating' on the palate – can be avoided by following a few simple rules. Firstly, always chop the onions as finely as possible. Secondly, if, for example, you are frying onions, cook them gently without letting them colour, until softened. Adding anything else to the pan will prevent the onions becoming completely soft. Finally, whatever cooking method you use – roasting, grilling, frying or boiling – always make sure the onions are thoroughly cooked.

If cooked properly, onions and garlic provide a rich but mild flavour that blends with other ingredients but never dominates.

For more than 5,000 years, people have recognized the wonderful properties of onions and garlic. Many cultures used garlic for its medicinal qualities. How reassuring to know that something so delicious is also good for you!

OILS AND VINEGARS

A bewildering range of oils is available nowadays and deciding which one to use for a particular dish can be far from easy. These are the guidelines I follow:

For shallow- and deep-frying and for grilling I use groundnut oil or a good vegetable oil. For Mediterranean vegetables, salads, fish and meat dishes, I use good-quality olive oil.

For dressings, the choice is made tricky by the vast range of speciality oils on the market – hazelnut, truffle, garlic, pumpkinseed, walnut, grapeseed and many more. Matching the right oil in the right dressing with the right food takes time and care. Some pairings work well, many others don't. Successful combinations include: wild mushrooms, delicate curly endive and corn salad with walnut oil; and asparagus with sherry vinegar and olive oil.

If you invest money in a good oil, your vinegar must be of equal quality. Again, the choice is vast. You can stock your shelves from a range of vinegars that includes tarragon, raspberry, red wine, cider, garlic, and pepper. The one to be avoided at all costs in salad dressings is malt vinegar. Be wary, too, of mixing a highly flavoured oil with a highly flavoured vinegar. As in every good marriage, only one partner can dominate at any one time!

COOKING FISH AND MEAT

Fish or meat, vegetable or fruit, with everything you cook there is a moment of perfection, when the food is tender and true, juicy and succulent. Making sure that moment is reached is the daily challenge of the chef. It can only be achieved if the produce you are using is fresh, of good quality, correctly seasoned and cooked at the right temperature for the right length of time.

All the cooking methods discussed below require the same care and attention to detail. Cooking fish is particularly demanding because it is so delicate. Time and temperature are absolutely crucial. Whether you fry, grill, steam or poach, always test the fish with the point of a knife. The flesh in the centre should still be slightly translucent and opaque.

Remember that fish and meat will continue to cook after you have taken the pan from the heat. The heat retained in the pan can be enough to overcook your dish so remove the fish or cut of meat as soon as you are sure it has reached that elusive perfect moment.

Roasting

Without any doubt, meat tastes best roasted in the traditional way as a large joint. Much of the success of well-roasted meat depends on the fat. Butchers who trim all but a sliver of fat from their joints are doing you no favour. High-quality meat should have a good percentage of fat, whether it is the wonderful yellow marbling inside a joint of beef or the outside covering of fat on pork and lamb. When you roast a joint, the fat melts and introduces moisture and flavour. To retain those succulent juices, all roasted meats should rest in a warm place for at least 15 minutes before carving.

But let's not rush ahead! The first step is to find a butcher you can trust. Make sure he knows you will accept only the best. Proper maturation is one of the guarantees of high quality. Beef should be aged for 21 days and lamb for 7. Recently the trend with game has been for a less pungent and 'gamey' flavour. As with all foods, this is a matter of personal taste. I hang pheasant for 3–4 days and partridge for 2–3. I do not hang grouse at all, as I believe its naturally strong flavour does not require it.

In the past, roasting joints in hotel kitchens was something of an art form – free expression was valued above the basic rules! Scant attention was paid to oven temperature, the clock or use of a temperature probe. Joints were thrown into the oven and pronounced done after a quick prod from a sous chef's finger. Those days are gone. I believe in leaving nothing to chance; I take great care to get the timing and temperature exactly right. Always remove meat from the refrigerator in good time. Allowing it to reach room temperature gradually and naturally will pay handsome dividends in terms of tenderness and juiciness.

Season the meat generously with salt and pepper. For poultry and game birds, it is very important to season inside as well as out. I am also very fond of using different stuffings for different birds – apple and sage for duck, onion, garlic and rosemary for chicken, apple and plum for goose, and thyme and onion for game birds.

I often spike leg or shoulder of lamb and leg or best end of pork with garlic cloves. Best end of lamb and saddle of lamb or beef have fine, delicate flavours that are best left alone, so I usually cook them in their natural state. The only exception I make is to sprinkle lamb with herbs, which I add towards the very end of the cooking process.

To roast meat, set your oven to 220°C/425°F/Gas Mark 7 and heat the roasting tin. There is no need for dripping. Add a little oil and turn the meat in the oil so that it is sealed all over. Don't use a fork as this will pierce the meat and release its precious juices.

For poultry, reduce the oven temperature to 200°C/400°F/Gas Mark 6 after exactly 10 minutes. I roast chicken for 15 minutes on each side, basting it frequently, and then for 30 minutes on its back. When you turn the chicken over, its juices should run clear. To test if the bird is done, insert a temperature probe 2cm/^{3}/$_4$ inch deep just above the thigh bone. A temperature of 80°C shows that the bird is cooked. Leave the meat to rest in a warm place for 10 minutes before you carve it.

When roasting duck, I cook it first for 20 minutes on each side, reducing the heat to 200°C/400°F/Gas Mark 6 after 10 minutes, and then on its back, for a total of 1¼ hours. I believe that roast duck should be well done but if you cook the breast off the bone, keep it pink.

Start game birds off in the same way as duck and chicken. I like grouse to be pink so I give it 6 minutes on each side at 230°C/450°F/Gas Mark 8. I feel the same about woodcock and snipe. For them 4 minutes on each side is enough. Pheasant needs about 10 minutes on each side. When you have completed this first stage of roasting for game birds, remove the protective fat from the bird's breast before turning it on its back. This will allow the breast to colour but not become dry.

Lean pieces of meat such as fillets of beef or veal and saddle or fillet of venison should be spiked with fat so that they do not dry out when they are roasted. For other joints, which have a layer of fat, this precaution is unnecessary.

Roasting meat until it loses its natural colour and turns a drab uniform grey should be a criminal offence! Pink is preferable by far.

For this reason, you need to keep a careful eye on meat right through the roasting process. Using a temperature probe will help ensure that it is cooked precisely how you like it.

Grilling and Frying

Grilling is a far healthier cooking method than frying since it requires very little fat. Some foods however, benefit from frying. To bring out the best in pork or sole, for example, I am willing to compromise my commitment to healthy eating and reach for the frying pan. The first rule when frying is to use a high-quality oil such as groundnut or sunflower. In the last quarter of the cooking time, add a little butter to give a golden colour and intensify the flavour.

Whether you are grilling or frying, the quality of meat you buy is crucial. Success also depends on careful timing. Just a few minutes too long in the pan or under the grill can turn even the best-quality meat or fish into a dried-out shadow of its former self.

If I am cooking a large piece of meat or fish, I often mark it on a ridged grill pan or fry it briefly to give it colour and flavour before transferring it to a baking tray to finish cooking in the oven at 200°C/400°F/Gas Mark 6.

I am no great friend of deep-frying, as it does not usually improve food. Quite the opposite! It can destroy the natural flavour and character of many ingredients. However, the exceptions to this are tempura, with its delicate crisp batter which is ideal for coating oysters, lobsters and vegetables, and wonton. Whenever you are deep-frying, always use the best oil available.

Steaming and Poaching

I have always been fond of steaming. The gentle heat preserves the colour and texture of the food, bringing out its natural flavour while retaining vitamins and minerals. At home I use a very old and battered couscousier. For fish, meat and vegetables, which need to be cooked delicately, this simple device is all you require.

Even the gentle heat of steaming has to be carefully controlled. Timing is of the essence, and a few minutes can make all the difference to the texture and freshness of the food.

I do not add herbs or any other flavourings to the water in the pan of my steamer, simply because I don't believe they have the slightest impact on the flavour of the food above. The very opposite is true of poaching. Everything you add to the stock or, for fish, to the court bouillon, has an impact on the taste of the food you are poaching. Getting the right balance of herbs, spices and vegetables is of the utmost importance, as too much or too little can spoil the end result.

Like steaming, poaching should be a gentle process. The finished stock should always be crystal clear, so it is well worth taking the time and trouble to make really good stocks.

Braising

Braising brings out the best in cuts of meat that have good fat cover and a high percentage of muscular tissue. These include shin of beef, oxtail, topside, chuck and silver side of veal.

Season the meat well, seal it all over in a casserole on the hob and then remove it from the dish. Brown some vegetables in the same dish and then add tomato purée, fresh tomatoes, wine, stock and herbs. Add some bones if you have them, to make the sauce you prepare from this mixture even richer. Return the meat to the casserole so that it is half covered by the stock. Put the lid on the casserole and place in an oven preheated to 180°C/350°F/Gas Mark 4. Braising is all about slow, gentle cooking; the slower the cooking the better the result. Make sure you baste and turn the meat frequently, and if the sauce is drying up, top it up with some stock. This will keep the meat moist and help produce a rich sauce full of character and flavour.

For large cuts, remove the lid for the final half hour so that the meat takes some colour. Braised meat must be well cooked so that the flesh falls easily from the bone.

COOKING VEGETABLES

Overcooking vegetables is like staying too long at a party – the best is already over, what's left is stale, tired and dull. Vegetables grown above ground should be crunchy. Lose that crisp texture and you lose the best of the vegetable in terms of colour, taste and nutrition. Vegetables grown underground should be cooked until they are tender but still firm. A potato turned to slurry from too long in the pan is a sorry sight.

Freshness is all. Vegetables are best eaten as soon as they are cooked. If there has to be a gap between kitchen and table, plunge the vegetables into plenty of ice-cold water. When you are ready to serve, reheat them with a little butter and a few spoonfuls of the liquid in which they were cooked. When the liquid has evaporated and the vegetables are coated in the butter, they will be – almost – as good as new.

BLANCHING AND REFRESHING

Blanching can be an excellent first step in the cooking process. It helps to maintain and intensify the colour, texture and flavour. It also preserves, sterilizes and removes impurities.

To blanch vegetables, shellfish and pasta, immerse them in salted boiling water. Drain and refresh them in iced water so the cooking process is stopped immediately.

To blanch bones or pieces of meat, cover them with cold water, bring it quickly to the boil and then drain and rinse in plenty of cold water.

Blanching helps preserve vitamins and minerals, since the food is cooked partially and very quickly. The next stage of cooking, if indeed one is needed, varies from dish to dish. For instance, with pasta you can reheat it with a little of the cooking liquid, butter or olive oil; with shellfish, remove the shells and then fry or grill them. Blanching langoustines takes 2–3 seconds, lobsters 3–4 minutes.

REDUCING

The definition of reducing is to lessen an amount of liquid by a specified amount by fast boiling to concentrate and intensify the flavour. It works wonders. Done correctly, reducing brings a depth and intensity of flavour to stocks and sauces. It is also an excellent way of thickening a stock or sauce until it achieves the perfect consistency for the dish you are preparing.

Be careful not to overseason. If the stock is highly seasoned before you begin reducing, it may be far too salty by the time you finish. Always ensure the stock is clear, not cloudy.

Stock made from poaching fish or meat can be delicious. When you have taken the meat or fish from the pan use the stock to make a sauce by adding cream, butter or a little flour.

Reducing can work wonders but it can't perform miracles. If your stock is poor to begin with, reducing will simply make it worse.

INDEX